HOW CAN I WORSHIP YOU, IF I CAN'T TRUST YOU?

Lamont McLaurin

Apologetics One

ISBN-13: 9781234567890
ISBN-10: 1477123456

Cover Design by: M.A. Jones Designs
Library of Congress Control Number: 2018675309
Printed in the United States of America

CONTENTS

Him?

FOREWORD

Being a survivor of child abuse, I've had many unanswered questions about God, and why He would allow such things to happen to a helpless child. Having the presence of mind as a child to pray, I was still left confused as to why one would still suffer such travail. In my childhood mind, I thought that once I began to pray, my situation would change, and my abuser would love me as the innocent child that I was.

My thinking was further from the truth. I spent my adolescence, teens and a part of my adult-life being verbally, mentally and at times physically abused by a parent hell-bent on showing me no love and offering no apology. Carrying that shame and physical scars into my adulthood, I needed answers.

Wrecked with sadness, low self-esteem, and worthlessness, I stumbled upon this audacious and riveting book, 'How Can I Worship You If I Can't Trust You,' written by Lamont McLaurin. He dares to ask the questions that many of us have pondered for years and have been told that it would be blasphemous to do so.

Page after page you will be enlightened by the male perceived perplexities of God. This theologian's page-turner will help transform your tragedies into triumph and answer some of life's most daunting questions about God.

Mr. McLaurin is not just a highly intelligent theologian but a polymath. His book will give you a better understanding of why you worship.

Written from a grateful heart,
KP

INTRODUCTION

Every human on the planet earth shares one common thread, and that is the desire to Worship something. Whether it is the God of the Bible, the Koran, or be it the sun, moon, stars, ocean, universe, statues, energy, ancestors, or the like, that particular entity must be held accountable for human suffering and make logical sense out of life.

'How Can I Worship You If I Can't Trust You' is a compilation of 30 short chapters. They read as a courtroom drama, with theologian Lamont McLaurin indicting the GOD of the universe in a multi-count indictment, in front of a jury pool of 12 atheists and an agnostic Judge.

This manuscript confronts the Creator of heaven and earth with a litany of daunting questions that appear to be of blasphemous nature, that religious leaders and most humans dare to inquire of God.

The results of this 21st Century Percocet will astonish the average reader.

CHAPTER 1: WORSHIP

◆ ◆ ◆

Worship is defined as "showing the reverence, adoration, love, devotion, or honor to a deity," or in simple terms, God.

The God of the Holy Bible, the God of Abraham, Isaac, and Jacob, never condemned atheism in the scriptures but condemned idol worship. The reason He did not condemn atheism is that atheism does not require worship. Additionally, atheism is described as an act of a retard or a fool. In Psalms 14:1, it says: "it's the fool that says in his heart that there is no God." Idol worship is a vastly different act. A person can knowingly, willingly, and intelligently know who the true and living God is, and purposely attribute his worship to an idol. I will give you two examples. One example took place approximately 3600 years ago in Egypt, the other was about five months ago in Philadelphia, Pennsylvania.

In the first example, the nation of Israel was in bondage for 430 years. God promised them a deliverer and that deliverer came in the form of Moses. When Moses met God, the first thing he asked Him was what His name was. The reason Moses asked God His name is because when God performed His miracles, He didn't want His worship and glory to be shared by another. This is why, when Moses went up on the mountain to worship God and didn't return in the time frame of their thinking, they collected the gold from their earrings and built a golden calf. They attributed every act, including plagues, parting of the Red Sea, etc., to a dumb, stupid idol that couldn't walk, talk, or breathe. As a result, 3000 were killed.

In the second example, approximately six months ago, I was working with one of my co-workers who is a female Muslim. While we are of different faiths, we had a particularly good social working relationship. On this particular day when she arrived at work, her countenance looked very sad and the spirit of grief was in the atmosphere. She began pacing back and forth and with an outburst, she cried, "my son, my only begotten son!" When I went to comfort her, I noticed that the word "begotten" began to resonate in my spirit. Moments later at the fax machine, a word dropped into my spirit. Now, I do not coin myself as a prophet or seer, but I know I heard from the true and living God!

While I knew the Lord's voice, I somewhat doubted the transmission of what came from His mouth to my spirit. The exact words were: "thus says the Lord, the God of Abraham, Isaac and Jacob, your son, your only begotten son, will do approximately two more years of jail time." At the time, my co-worker's son had been sentenced to life and had already served 16 years. When I prophetically spoke to her, I stated it verbatim, just as the Lord gave it to me. She looked at me with the expression of, "ok, thanks, but it is what it is."

Approximately two days later, on a Thursday night, I got a strange call from that co-worker. I exchanged greetings as she began screaming, "you will never believe what happened!" I said, "What?" She replied, "Everything you said to the very letter came to pass, I mean every single word!" Then in Arabic, she said, "Alhamdulillah," which means "thanks" to the God of the Quran.

Now as a reader, what's wrong with that picture? Here is what's wrong: the woman was in travail for 16 years due to her only "begotten" son being incarcerated. One day she cries out and a Christian gives her a word from God, and 48 hours later upon the fruition of that word, with unbelievable accuracy, her worship and glory are offered to a God (Allah) who had absolutely nothing to do with the manifestation of the miracle, nor was he petitioned in the prayer.

Imagine a man working three jobs consistently for 30 years to pay for his children's college education. Throughout the 30 years, the man was hospitalized several times and suffered many ailments. Meanwhile, his children had a stepfather who offered no support, and showed no interest or respect to the children at all. At the graduation ceremony which proved to be the happiest day of the biological father's life, he sat patiently on the edge of his seat, anticipating the announcement of the parent who labored and supported their children through college. His child began to give his speech and pledged all credit, glory, and accolades to the stepfather. One could only imagine the hurt, pain, and disappointment the father experienced. As it is with God.

The apostle John wrote in John 4:24, "God is a spirit, and they that worship him must worship him in spirit and truth." One might ask, "What is the purpose of worship?"

Worship has several purposes and I will elaborate on the three most distinct enumerated below.

1) To usher in God's presence
2) To thank God for His acts
3) To give peace to the human spirit

Let's discuss first the ushering of God's spirit by contrasting the subject of the human spirit. Simply because we are made in God's image and likeness, we have similarities and commonalities alike.

When a man is attempting to get a woman's attention that he is extremely fond of and he is going out on a date with her, the man first communicates with her to examine her likes and dislikes. Once he has that lined up, he puts on his best apparel, makes sure his teeth are brushed, his hair is groomed, and his vehicle is cleaned inside and out. Likewise, the woman, whether virtuous or carnal, will emulate the same type of behavior – hair done, clothes fitted, make-up done to perfection, sweet-smelling perfume, and the like. Ok author, what's your point? My point is, humans are spirit beings and as spirit beings, we naturally and intrinsically know how to get the attention of the opposite sex for a particular purpose. Same with God, but He is NOT human but a spirit. And the Bible shows believers exactly how to get his attention for a particular purpose. In 2nd Chronicles chapter 20, God gives a wonderful illustration of how to entreat and invoke His presence. When you read verses 1 and 2, this begins the entreating of God's presence, drama, or tribulation.

The character Jehoshaphat heard a rumor that would soon become fact. Three vicious nations set their sights to destroy the people of God. The first act Jehoshaphat did was to call a fast for all the believers. Fasting humbles your spirit. Scripture says: "God resists the proud but comes near the humble." The second thing he did was to hallow God. Watch this: and Jehoshaphat said, "O Lord God of our fathers, are thou not God in heaven; And rules over all the kingdoms of the nonbeliever? And in thine hand, is there power and might so that there is none who could stand against You?"

Jehoshaphat identified who God was, where He was located, and what He could do. Then in verse 18, the Bible says: "He bent down his face to the ground and began worshiping the Lord." Wow! When you continue to read, it states then "the spirit of the Lord" came in the midst. As the three vicious nations were preparing to attack Israel, God mysteriously turned them on one another, and Israel not only prevailed but inherited their finances after they began slaughtering one another.

If you read the Bible you will come across several different names of God – Jehovah Rohi, Jehovah Shammah, Jehovah Rophe, and many more. Why all the names? The reason God has so many names is that in the Old Testament prophets erected an altar to God as a memorial of His acts every time they had an issue or crisis that God resolved or delivered them out of.

Finally, worship is not just for God, it's for the believers as well. When a human worships God, there is a shift in the atmosphere because you have just changed realms. In the earthly realm, it has a language (you are doomed, there is no hope, give up, it's impossible, etc.). When the realm shifts, so does the language (anything you ask in my name I will do, for with God nothing is impossible, I will show you great and mighty things that you do not know). Because of the shift of realms, your spiritual condition immediately shifts – no more stress, depression, or uneasiness, just peace.

Recently I was having a conversation with an old friend named Gregory Flamer that I used to work with at the police department. He shared with me that he had congestive heart failure. After our countless conversations and during my meditation time, I would think to myself, "Wow, not just heart failure, but cancer too." I wondered how I would deal with heart failure alone. Like clockwork six months later, I suffered a heart attack in church right after service. I was rushed to the hospital and I overheard an Indian physician say, "It's CHF." I responded, "Doc, what is CHF?" He replied, "congestive heart failure." I was visibly shaken for about an hour.

At some point, I was admitted to the hospital. God began to whisper in my spirit, "Worship Me!" Right after my worship, my cardiologist, who had a horrendous bedside manner, came into my room. He began to rob me of all hope I had for living with words that detailed what happened to five of my closest friends, who had all died from congestive heart failure. Like clockwork, the doctor said to me, "You are 56 years old; you have hypertension and a low injection fracture (I.F), which normally is 55 to 60. Your I.F is 19! Therefore, your heart muscle that pumps the blood is so weak that you could die if you sneeze." He further said, "praying is nice, but we live in the real world, in real-time, and the hard fact is, you are going to die." I looked at him dead in his eyes and replied, "I like those odds!"

Every morning between the hours of 8 am and noon, the cardiologist would come into my room with a team of interns and would ask the same rhetorical question: "How are you doing, Mr. McLaurin?" I would respond, "I never had a bad day in my life." The interns would look at one another, knowing that the diagnosis on the chart said something markedly different from my testimony. Every day for approximately two weeks, this standard daily ritual was recited all day, every day, to the extent that the doctors would come in my room reciting it themselves in unison:

"I never had a bad day in my life!"

Approximately one month later, the cardiologist set me up for an echocardiogram, which essentially is an ultrasound for the heart. The echo revealed that my I.F. remained the same at 19. I was then given about eight different medications, of which I only took two because of the draconian side effects. Again, I was told: "It doesn't look good, the bad news is you are going to die any day now. The good news is, it will be quick, and you will not suffer." In faith, and with a huge smile on my face I stated, "I like those odds."

One day while driving down Baltimore Pike, I began to have a conversation with God. I said, "God, death is not in my spirit. Since it isn't, what are we going to do?" He replied, "Strengthen your heart muscle." I replied, "How?" He replied, "The same way you weakened it." I chuckled and said, "Deep!" I began a light regiment of exercise and I told God that the next time I see the doctors, I would like my echo to read I.F. 35. I promised God that I would do cartwheels down Broad Street if He made that happen.

Three months later, I entered the doctor's office which was filled with sick and hopeless people. The receptionist said, "Hello Mr. McLaurin, how are you?" I responded, "Sensational! I never had a bad day in my life." I looked around the waiting room and it was almost like a spirit of life had resurrected every human being in the room.

As I entered the room to take my test, I began to worship silently. When the test was concluded, the technician said, "Wow! I can't believe it. Wow! Wow!" I replied, "Can't believe what?" He said, "Your I.F. was 48." I said, "Jumping Jiminy crickets! Lord, I asked for a 35, not for you to cause the machine to be recalibrated." The doctor came in and said, "This cannot be possible. Something is wrong with the machine." I smiled and walked out of the office, turned and looked at him and said, "I told you I liked those odds."

Six months later, I was advised by my primary doctor to consider bariatric weight loss surgery to assist with attaining a healthy weight for better heart health. During pre-op testing, the x-ray of my abdomen revealed an eight-centimeter cyst on one of my kidneys. I dropped my head and immediately thought of my friend Greg. Heart failure and cancer. Three weeks later it was confirmed that it was cancerous. Immediately I heard a voice that said to me, "Keep the matter a secret and worship your way through this ordeal." It was a difficult thing to do, because I had just lost one of my best friends, William Wingate, to cancer. Nevertheless, I put my "Go Hard" boots on and I raised that banner: "I never had a bad day in my life."

Another month later while being prepped for surgery, my cardiologist stopped by my room. He asked me with empathy, "Are you ok? I read your chart and you have only a seven percent chance at beating this." (I also knew these odds because I had recently watched a study on YouTube conducted by a Johns Hopkins University research team.) I looked at him with a huge Kool-Aid smile and said, "I like those odds." As he walked away shaking his head, he spoke the infamous words of non-believers, "good luck." Moments later I went into surgery worshipping inwardly, came out of surgery still worshipping inwardly, cancer gone, no chemotherapy, no ringing of the bells, just worship.

Worship is not exclusively for God; it is for you!

"Seek the Lord and his strength, seek his face continually."

1 CHRONICLES 16:11

CHAPTER 2: TEN COFFINS AND YOU WANT WORSHIP?

◆ ◆ ◆

"While he was yet speaking, there came also another and said, thy sons and thy daughters were eating and drinking wine in their eldest brother's house. And behold there came a great wind from the wilderness, and smote the four corners of the house, and it fell apart on the young men, and they're dead; and I only am escaped alone to tell thee. Then Job arose, and rent his mantle, and shaved his head, and fell down upon the ground, and worshipped."

JOB 1:18-20

When God first introduced the character of Job, he gave a very descriptive portfolio. God started by describing Job's character. God said, "Job was perfect, upright, hated evil, and feared God." God also said that Job had ten children: seven sons and three daughters. Job was what is considered a billionaire in today's standards. Last but not least, God said through His Holy Spirit that Job offered sacrifices to God continually just in case his children sinned against God.

Now I go back to the title of this chapter, "Ten Coffins and You Want Worship?" Prior to Job receiving this horrific news, some previous reports had Job devastated. His servants were killed, his oxen were stolen and the fire from heaven (probably a lightning bolt) burned up the sheep and the rest of the servants. So basically, in one day Job went broke, lost all of his children, and the first thing he did was worship.

What was in the mind of Job at that time? Was Satan having a conversation with him? Absolutely! I guess Job said, "God said I was perfect, just, upright, fearful of Him, and I hate evil. It wasn't enough that I went from billionaire to welfare all in one day, but he took my children after I made sure they were good in His sight because I sacrificed continually for them. Why me? What did I do wrong? I did everything right. What part of the game is this?" Worship is not a response to what God has done for you; worship is a response to who God is.

After all these things, Job's first words were, "Naked came I out of my mother's womb and naked I shall return; the Lord gave and the Lord has taken away; blessed be the name of the Lord." Job had a profound understanding of nothing from nothing equals nothing. You see, when God gave you life, before conception you were nothing. So whether you are Bill Gates, Donald Trump, a person in a homeless shelter, a blue-collar worker, or working paycheck to paycheck, you are indebted to God to ascribe worship to HIM and HIM alone.

The devil said something very telling to God. He asked, "Does Job worship you for nothing? Put forth your hand to all of his blessings and you will see the real Job." The devil had a valid point. We, meaning believers, even non-believers could get a new job and would proclaim, "God is good," settle a lawsuit, "God is a provider," receive healing, "God is faithful." But who is He when you are sick and close to death? Who is He when your finances are low? Who is He when your house is being foreclosed on? Who is He when you've prayed for your marriage to get better only to receive divorce papers in the mail? Not only who is He, but can you worship Him?

Job's wife was a classic example of a conditional believer. This was her response to Job's situation: "Do thy still retain thy integrity, why don't you curse God and die?" Job's wife was no different from your average believer today. If God has a hedge around you, He is worthy of worship. The day the hedge is removed, you want to curse God and die. Why is this verse in Job 2:9 so dangerous and revelatory at the same time? If you curse God and die, His worship stops. What is Satan's angle to get you to direct your worship to him or stop it completely?

Here are the questions at bar. Why is Satan so hell-bent on

stopping your worship? And why does God allow it? It seems like "it's" a conspiracy.

The reason why Satan is hell-bent on directing your worship towards him or stopping your worship of God altogether is that Satan has been where you are going, and he has been eternally cast out. Satan knows that worship brings in the presence of God. Everything that comes into God's presence must yield to Him, whether it is cancer, foreclosure, dysfunctional families, lack, etc. God, on the other hand, uses this opportunity to reveal Himself through your trials. Example: How would you know that God is a healer if it wasn't for diabetes? How would you know God is a provider if it wasn't for lack? How would you know that God is a God of peace if it wasn't for the unrest? Then when He reveals Himself through miracles as a result of your worship, your worship is taken to another level. You see Him differently, so you say "Hallelujah" differently, you cry and call His name differently, you pray differently, and you even discuss Him differently. Worship is produced from a heart that is broken. Troubled times break the heart and the enemy knows it, but so does God.

Something else that the enemy and God know is your expected end. While the enemy doesn't know the future, he does know God. Not by faith, but person to person. He knows God's character. God's character is His faithfulness. God demonstrated His faithfulness in Job not only by restoring what he lost but by giving him back everything doubled.

Job's perspective of God was clear. By faith he knew God would bring him to an expected end, so although he was broke, sick, and childless, he still counted God faithful. In the end, he received double and God received worship so great that it probably shook the heavens.

> "There hath no temptation taken you but such as is common to man: but God is faithful, who will not suffer you to be tempted above that ye are able; but will with the temptation also make a way to escape, they may be able to bear it."

1 CORINTHIANS 10:13

CHAPTER 3: EVEN THE DOGS

◆ ◆ ◆

In the book of Matthew chapter 15 verses 21-28, Jesus encountered a woman with a pressing issue: her daughter was possessed by a demon. Today it would be like your son or daughter on drugs. Jesus' dialogue was very peculiar insomuch that He turned the woman away not once but twice. To make matters worse, after turning her away two times He called her a dog! Now, theologically, people from other walks of faith read that chapter and say the Bible was altered because Jesus' words weren't indicative of His character. Jesus did not speak in that manner. But after careful observation, they are proven wrong. These were Jesus' actual words and through His actions, He was setting up a miracle and not being mean spirited.

Let's look at it from the onset. A woman from the coast of Tyre and Sidon who wasn't a Jew went up to Jesus and cried out to Him, "Lord Son of David." That was tantamount to calling Jesus God. Now after she hallowed Him, He still didn't answer her (He was testing her faith). However, when He does answer her, He said, "I have been sent only to the lost sheep of Israel."

After that devastating blow, the Bible says she began to worship Him. After she finished worshipping Him, He said, "It is not right to take the children's blessings and give them to little dogs." Instead of the woman saying, "to hell with this, it is what it is," or just sheepishly walking away, she said, "Truth Lord, but even the little dogs eat the crumbs from the master's table."

Now let's look at this woman's statement which caused Jesus to practically lose his mind with excitement. Her first response to Jesus was, "True." She acknowledged that she was a "dog," and this is the mystery throughout the Bible in Exodus 11:7, Matthew

7:6, Philippians 3:2, and Revelation 22:15. In all of them, God refers to humanity as dogs. The reason God does this is not to insult humans, but to illustrate that human character is consistent with a dog's character apart from the law. Foreigners didn't have laws. Example: Take ten dogs of any species, give them each a bowl of food and a bowl of water, and then leave the room unattended. What do you think will happen in that room? It will disrupt in utter chaos! Although each dog has equal portions, they will fight one another to the death despite having such. The same would be the situation with humans. If you rid the world of law enforcement for one week, just imagine the chaos and debauchery that would ensue. We would act like dogs in an unattended room of food. When Jesus heard the woman's response with diligence and persistence behind it, He no longer revered her as a dog. He instead said, "O woman great is your faith, be it unto you anything that you want." And her daughter was healed that very hour.

The Bible is clear in Hebrews 11:6 where it says, "but without faith it is impossible to please Him, for he that cometh to God must believe that He is and that He is a rewarder of them that diligently seek Him." The operative word in this verse is "diligent." This woman's faith was the portrait of diligence. She told Jesus who He was (Son of David, which means the Messiah), and when she was denied she would not walk away from God's face. The deep part was that she wasn't even a Jew.

Whenever you are in worship, you must believe and take it seriously. Although you are physically and geographically placed, your spirit has traveled to another realm. In this realm you are in the presence of the true and living God. As you begin to worship Him, He is going to test you to see if you believe the things you confess to believe. This is why your worship must be by devotion and not duty, in spirit and truth. You may ask, what is spirit and truth? This woman was not a Jew and supposedly didn't know God, but when she came to Jesus, she properly identified Him. She didn't ask Him if He was the Son of God, she declared that He was the Son of God. And that was the truth. She cried the issue out of her spirit and then she began to worship that which she said out of her mouth. Wow!

"O come, let us worship and bow down: let us kneel before the Lord our maker."

PSALM 95:6

CHAPTER 4: I'M NOT TRYING TO HEAR IT

◆ ◆ ◆

"We are troubled on every side, yet not distressed; we are perplexed, but not in despair; Persecuted, but not forsaken; cast down, but not destroyed."

2 CORINTHIANS 4:8

Have you ever experienced a season of tribulation in your finances, social life, health, etc.? Just a space of time when your life is met with challenge after challenge. There comes a time when you are predicting an end and there are signs that this nightmare is almost over. You begin to put it into expectation and the rug is pulled right from under you. You picked out prayer partners that you know can touch glory, and now you are cast down and perplexed. Lord, what are you doing? Lord, what happened? Lord why? Lord are you for real?

Your prayer partners feel that lightning is supposed to strike for you that day and they text you, "So give me the praise report!" You respond, "I didn't get it," or, "I was denied." They respond, "God has something better for you," "God didn't want that for you," "It wasn't God's time," "God knew you weren't ready," etc. Agreeably you respond, "I know, thanks. Praise the Lord anyhow." But on the inside, you are saying, "I'm not trying to hear that, I fasted, I prayed, I lived something, I believed. I'm not trying to hear that."

Often in a believer's life, you run into faith situations that leave you feeling perplexed and in despair. Because you and your prayer partners can't figure out God's ways on your issue, the intercessor begins to give out what I coin as "dark counsel." Dark counsel: when a believer attempts to console another believer but doesn't give them what God said. In the believers' spirit man, they are somewhat disturbed by the undertaking and they say to themselves, "I'm not trying to hear it."

The problem with dark counsel is that, while your intentions are good, it doesn't un-ring the bell. Nine times out of ten while you feel for the person in the affliction, you cannot share in their physical pain so it's easy to say, "It's all good, everything is going to be all right. Praise him anyhow," when at its taproot, they have to carry the burden alone. They are in the fire and you are not.

Recently my season of several issues that I was believing for a turnaround ended. I was excited and filled with expectations, then on that day, boom! The rug was pulled from under me. Like clockwork the intercessors were texting, "Hey man of God, give us a praise report." When I responded thumbs down, they responded, "It's going to be ok, the Lord has a better plan for you." As kind and sweet-sounding as those words were, it did not take away the despair or the perplexing thoughts in my heart. I simply said, "Thanks, but I'm not trying to hear it." Later that day I received my breakthrough and it came from my son, Lamont. He patted me on my back and then walked away shaking his head. His response was eerily comforting. It was almost as if he felt my pain, my angst, my discomfort.

Nevertheless, I worshipped God through the trial and approximately 45 days later, lightning struck. My expectations were fulfilled. Delayed doesn't mean denied. Being brutally honest, at the time of expectation I wasn't trying to hear it.

On many occasions, believers can be disingenuous about a faith trial or their spiritual journey with God. They begin to mask their pain supposing they are being spiritual, but that is an unhealthy relationship with God. God said in Isaiah 1:18, "Come now, let us reason together..." Jesus said in Matthew 11:28-29, "Come unto me, all he that labor and are heavy laden, and I will give you rest. Take my yoke upon you and learn of me; for I am meek and lowly in heart: and ye shall find rest unto your souls."

So, the import is that while God is holy, almighty, righteous, and the like, He is also knowable, personal, intimate, and emotional. So, there is an expectancy of the Almighty to listen to you vent your emotions, concerns, and displeasures. It's one of the greatest acts of faith because at its taproot, you are either crazy or you are having an intelligent conversation with an invisible God.

In conclusion, while I know you're not trying to hear it, faith comes by hearing and He is a rewarder of those who diligently seek Him. So, after you've vented, cried, and meditated on the situation, know that delayed doesn't mean denied and God is faithful even when we are faithless. You heard!

"So then faith cometh by hearing and hearing by the word of God."

ROMANS 10:17

CHAPTER 5: IF I HEAR ANOTHER PROPHECY, I WILL SCREAM!

◆ ◆ ◆

"Hope deferred maketh the heart sick: but when the desire cometh, it is a tree of life."

PROVERBS 13:12

The Bible says, "hope deferred (wishing or anticipating something) maketh the human heart sick." What exactly is a sick heart? A sick heart is a heart filled with hope and expectancy for a particular desire or want. When hope is "deferred" (putting something off until a later time) the heart can begin to get sick. When something alive is sick, it doesn't function properly. When it comes to humans, the sickness comes in the form of depression, anxiety, stress, isolation, and the like.

When a worshipper petitions God, the worshipper is told to believe by faith. When God answers a prayer, He answers prayer according to His counsel of His will. One might ask, what is the counsel of His will? When a worshipper prays, he or she ends their prayer with "amen." The word "amen" is universally recognized as believing the person is simply saying, "I'm signing off" or "that's all." By ending a prayer with the word "amen," we are simply saying "according to Your perfect will." It is a marvelous reminder that any discussion about prayer must begin with the understanding that we are conforming to God's will, not He to ours. Because God is outside of creation, He knows the end from the beginning so He responds according to what He sees and not what we can't see.

When ministering to a sick heart, one must minister patience, faith, and hope. That is the only way a sick heart is stabilized. One dangerous thing that can cause what I coin as "congestive heart failure" is a false prophecy.

> When a prophet speaketh in the name of the LORD, if the thing follow not, nor come to pass, that is the thing which the LORD hath not spoken, but the prophet hath spoken it presumptuously: thou shalt not be afraid of him.
>
> DEUTERONOMY 18:22

When the Lord spoke to Israel about identifying a prophet, He set the bar in Deuteronomy 18:22. If a prophet (deacon, pastor, evangelist, bishop, etc.) professes something in the name of the Lord and it isn't followed by signs or come to pass, that person has lied to you.

It's one thing to tarry and wait for God, it's quite another thing to lie to a person and tell them God said it and they turn around and believe it and it leaves them three times worse than they were in the beginning. God took prophecy so serious in the Old Testament that the penalty was death to anyone who practiced giving out false prophecies.

In the book of Amos 8:11, the Bible says, "there will be a famine for the word of God." My personal belief is that we are living in it today.

On Facebook there is a post from Bishop Jakes that says, if you send this chain message to ten people, tomorrow God is going to give you $70,000. Nice message, very hopeful, but I sent it and I'm broke. Someone tells you, "The Lord said in 60 days you are going to meet your spouse." Nice message, very hopeful, but it's been two years and I'm still lonely. They tell you, "The Lord said that new position on your job, claim it and it is yours." You claimed it last month and this month you get laid off. "If I hear another prophecy I'm going to scream!" The danger with uttering false prophecies is that the person never considers the mind of God. They never consider seasons, God's counsel, God's predetermination, or His will. The only thing they consider is getting you out of the hole that God allowed you to be in for His special purpose.

You have been to women's/men's conferences, walking by faith and empowerment conferences, and most times you attend looking for a move or a word from God. Sometimes you get one, but often your anxiety is so high you lose sight of discernment. And whatever the guest speaker speaks into your life, you're off to the races and within days, weeks, or months when nothing comes to fruition, you say that all too familiar saying in your heart: "If I hear another prophecy I will scream."

God has warned His people in Proverbs 4:23 to "guard your heart with diligence." Why? Because it can get sick if it doesn't receive the right counsel. When Job went through his trial, three men, Eliphaz, Bildad, and Zophar, came to minister to him. All of these men seemed to speak with great wisdom, yet they didn't have a clue of what God was dealing with in Job. It was to the point that God said His wrath was kindled against Eliphaz and his two friends. Why? Because they didn't speak of the Lord, the thing that was right, but Job did. (Job 42:7)

In conclusion, every worshipper like Job has an expected end. There are times when you don't want to hear from Bishop Jakes, Creflo Dollar, Bishop Evans, or your pastor. All you want to hear is the Lord say, "Thus says the Lord."

"Remember the former things of old: for I am God, and there is none else; I am God and there is none like me, declaring the end from the beginning, and from ancient times the things that are not yet done, saying, my counsel shall stand, and I will do all my pleasure: calling a ravenous bird from the east, that man that executeth my counsel from a far country: yea, I have spoken it, I will also bring it to pass; I have purposed it, I will also do it."

ISAIAH 46:9-11

CHAPTER 6: LORD, YOU LIED

◆ ◆ ◆

"No weapon formed against thee shall prosper; and every tongue that shall rise against thee in judgment thou shalt condemn. This is the heritage of the servants of the Lord, and their righteousness is of me, saith the LORD."

ISAIAH 54:17

The scene is Emanuel African Methodist Church in Charleston, South Carolina; the date is June 17, 2015. On a warm summer evening, ten believers of various ages have come together to worship God. The pastor preached a full sermon on Isaiah 54:17, and right in the middle of the service, a young man named Dylann Roof, who was possessed by the devil, entered the church with a Glock 41.45 handgun. He instantly began shooting, hitting all ten worshippers, killing nine of them.

Putting aside the trauma and anxiety, the lone survivor began to meditate on the events of the evening and the word of God, focusing on Isaiah 54:17. Only one conclusion this worshipper can come to and that is, "God, You lied." And to be even more transparent (I apologize if I stepped on some religious toes), most of your religious leaders, bishops, prophets, evangelists, and a bevy of other church officials are silently asking the same question in the vicissitudes of their hearts. Others are openly saying it by employing security agents to do what they believe God failed at or appeared to have failed at.

At its taproot, while this was a tragic attack, it was an attack on faith, not a race. While my import is not to be insensitive to the people involved or affected by the tragedy, the pure intent of the enemy was to make God appear as a liar. And if he is successful at planting that seed of doubt in your heart, he then can uproot faith and cause you to DIS-BELIEVE the word of God. This attack or trick is not new. It is as old as the Garden of Eden. And while it is archaic it has not lost its luster, John the Baptist was tempted by it, as well as Jeremiah, Habakkuk, Moses, David, Daniel, and a pantheon of other men of faith. Just like past experiences, God always proves Himself faithful.

Many people have weighed in on this incident from all walks of life and religions. But one commentary that appealed to my theological mental assent was when a pastor by the name of Dr. Miles of Philadelphia, Pennsylvania, made this simple but brilliant statement: "The answer is not the answer." Exactly what did this pastor mean? What she meant was, it's a mystery with incomprehensible elements to it, in short, or simplified terms. Something happened unexpectedly, unforeseen, and tragic of which we don't know why, and in our feeble attempts to reason the unknowable we come up with the theories that are somewhat comforting but not settling to the human heart. In other words, it doesn't un-ring the bell, it still hurts, and even more, it is still PERPLEXING.

When Job was at the apex of his suffering and the Almighty was about to heal him, the Almighty did something highly intelligent. Instead of giving Job an answer for his suffering, He had Job turn the focus of his suffering to God's majesty. The Almighty began by asking Job some particularly important questions like, "Where were you when I laid the foundation of the earth? When the morning stars sang together, where were you? Who set the guidelines of the waves and said come no further, and by His word it comes no further? Have thou perceived the breadth of the earth, declare it if you know? Does the rain have a father, tell me if you know? Who put the breeze in the trees, where does it come from, does it have a gardener?"

Job responded to God and said, "I know you can do everything, therefore I uttered things too lofty for me that I knew not." Moments after concentrating on God's majesty, providence, and

21

glory, he repented himself and God restored to him double of everything he lost.

Scripture says in Numbers 23:19, "God is not a man, that He should lie; neither the son of man, that He should repent: hath He said, and shall He not do it? Or hath He spoken, and shall He not make it good?"

Frequently when we read scripture, we discern it emotionally. Huge mistake. Scripture says in 1 Peter 2:2: "...desire the sincere milk of the word." In other words, read scripture for all it is worth, allowing the Spirit to give you the literal interpretation of what God is saying.

When the South Carolina tragedy occurred, the main scripture that popped into the believer's minds was Isaiah 54:17, "No weapon formed against thee shall prosper." In the average believer's mind, including yours truly, we ponder God's word, the facts of the case. Human reasoning says, "Hey God, I know you are good, righteous, holy, and a whole lot of other positive attributes, but what happened in this situation?" The answer: God's word did not and cannot fail. The church has misunderstood that verse and has discerned it emotionally. Let us look at a rightful interpretation of that scripture through some others.

> And in her was found the blood of prophets, and of saints, and of all that were slain upon the earth.
>
> REVELATIONS 18:24

> O Jerusalem, Jerusalem, thou that killest the prophets and stoniest them that are sent unto thee....
>
> MATTHEW 23:37

Question: How were these prophets killed?

Answer: 2nd Corinthians 10:4 and Ephesians 6:11-12 – i.e., by the sword, stoned, hanged, etc. Are swords, stones, and ropes weapons? The answer: yes. So clearly God could not have been talking about a physical weapon. If He wasn't talking about a physical weapon, then what type of weapon was He talking about?

> For the weapons of our warfare are not carnal, but mighty through God to the pulling down of strongholds.
>
> 2 CORINTHIANS 10:4

> Put on the whole armor of God, that ye may be able to stand against the wiles of the devil. For we wrestle not against flesh and blood, but against principalities, against powers, against the rulers of the darkness of this world, against spiritual wickedness in high places.
>
> EPHESIANS 6:12

The weapons that God is talking about are spiritual weapons that speak to you daily. Example: Does God have enough mercy to forgive this sin? I'm not going to go to church because I fornicated. God doesn't hear my prayer. I'm not going to pray because He doesn't answer anyway. God is going to get me because I missed church today. All of these statements are lies, and the weapon used against these is the sword of the Spirit which is the word of God.

Eternal life doesn't begin at death; rather, it begins the moment you have accepted Christ as your Lord and Savior. Death has a perfect statistic; you only get one per person. In our eyes, the South Carolina incident was a horrific tragedy, but what if the nine that were translated went to another dimension and are experiencing something so awesome that when they think about us, they begin to tear up? While we don't have all of the answers, we have to lean on what is exclusive. For something to be exclusive, it has to be first provable, knowable, and absolute.

When Jesus spoke, He spoke like no other so-called prophet on this earth. He didn't say, "I know the truth," rather He said, "I am the truth." He didn't say, "I know the way," rather, He said, "I am the way." He never said there is a resurrection, rather He said, "I am the resurrection." Not only did He say all of these bold statements, but He also turned around and proved every assertion. Most people confuse truth and opinion. However, that couldn't be further from the truth. An opinion is a way you view a thing, while the truth is a core set of facts that are consistent with reality or are provable. An opinion is a feeling, truth is a fact.

In conclusion, the God of the Bible always gives a standard for belief. Jesus said in the book of Matthew 24:35: "Heaven and earth shall pass away, but my words shall not pass away."

"God is not a man, that He should lie; neither the son of man, that He should repent: hath He said, and shall He not do it? Or hath He spoken, and shall He not make it good?"

NUMBERS 23:19

CHAPTER 7: THOU HE SLAY ME...

◆ ◆ ◆

Thou He slay me, yet will I trust him: but I will maintain mine own ways before Him.

JOB 13:15

In the book of Job, as Job was passing through tribulation, he uttered that verse out of the vicissitudes of his heart. Job accused God of slaying him. The word "slay," according to Merriam Webster dictionary, means "to violently kill with premeditation." Job's tribulation was so intense, he used this verse to describe the magnitude of his pain. Although it was Satan who was afflicting him, he charged God because he knew that God was in control.

Often in a worshipper's life, there is a feeling of disparity, hopelessness, forsakenness, etc. Scripture tells us in 2nd Corinthians 4:8-9: "We are troubled on every side, yet not distressed; we are perplexed, but not in despair; persecuted, but not forsaken; cast down, but not destroyed." What was the complaint of Job then and what is the complaint of the worshipper today when it comes to feeling slayed, perplexed, and cast down? When a worshipper begins to feel these emotions it is because he or she looked at the word of God, looked at the promises in the word, and compared the word with the present condition or state that they are in. Then the games begin. Examples: 1st Peter 5:7 says, "casting all your care upon him; for He careth for you." Read that scripture, pray on it, get up off your knees from worship, and when you open your eyes, you're in the dark because the electric company turned off your power.

> *"Blessed is the man that walketh not in the counsel of the ungodly, nor standeth in the way of sinners, nor sitteth in the seat of the scornful. But his delight is in the law of the LORD; and in his law doth he meditate day and night. And shall he be like a tree planted by the rivers of water that bringeth forth his fruit in his season; his leaf also shall not wither; and whatsoever he doeth shall prosper."*
>
> PSALM 1:1-2

You have read the Psalm and you've applied it to your life. Don't hang with the ungodly, give to the poor, preach the gospel to the homeless, and yet the person on your job that lives like Satan just got the promotion that you were qualified for. The ending of that scripture says: "And whatsoever he does he shall prosper."

At that point, a worshipper begins to feel like God is slowly killing them, intentionally. Although it's a feeling that cannot be described, it is something that has to be experienced.

The emotion of being slayed is exclusive only for the worshipper of God. An ordinary believer does not have the right to feel slayed. God said in 1st Peter 2:20, "For what glory is it, if when you be buffeted for your faults, ye shall take it patiently? But if, when ye do well, and suffer for it, ye take it patiently, this is acceptable with God." Now it's a different thing when you are living something for God, bringing Him glory, hoping in the word, and in its "appearance" the word fails. Then in your heart, you say, "Thou He slay me, yet I will trust in Him."

Question: How can you trust someone who has failed you? The answer: Easy.

When reciting Job 13:15, most people only recite part of the verse. The blessing is at the end of the verse which states: "I will surely defend my way to His face." Wow! Job appeared to be spiritually arrogant and he had justification for doing so. You might be saying, "Wait a minute, humble yourself, don't go there." My response would be, "I'm biblically sound to test the word of God."

In the introduction of Job 1, it is God, not a man, who described Job. God said that Job was spiritually upright, simply perfect in his ways, hated evil, and feared God. Job was living something. How do we know? Did the apostle say it, did the deacon say it, did the bishop say it? No, God said it. In Joshua 1:8 it says and guarantees, "This book of the law shall not depart out of thy mouth; but thou shalt meditate therein day and night, that thou mayest observer to do according to all that is written therein: for then thou shalt make thy way prosperous, and then thou shalt have good success." Ten coffins, bankruptcy, cancer, and homelessness all in one day is certainly not God's meaning of prosperity or success. Job out of his complaint said something very arrogant: "I will surely defend my way to His face." Wow! What in the ham n' cheese was Job saying to God?

The book of Revelation speaks about the 24 elders. They were the prophets and the disciples, the ones that brought God's word through The Holy Spirit on to this earth. Job was, in essence, saying, "Lord if you fail me and leave me in this condition after what you promised me in Joshua 1:8, and I've fulfilled my part in Joshua 1:8, I am going to hold court in heaven and expose you as a tyrannical fraud." God in His response told Job to put on the brakes. He asked some very pointed questions: "Where were you when I laid the foundation of the earth? Who shut up the sea's doors when it breaks forth? Who measured the earth with its dimensions?" God ignored the idol threats that Job made about holding court in heaven; rather, He had Job concentrate on His majesty. When Job concentrated on the majesty of God, it trumped all of his issues and caused him to worship. God asked Job a very acerbic question that no worshipper can escape: "Shall he that contend with the Almighty instruct him? He that reproved God, let him answer it."

The end result is that God is not blind. He sees your travail; He knows the end from the beginning. He wants the worshipper to continually gaze on Him, not their condition. The latter is always going to trump the former and the slaying is only to bring you to an expected end.

"For I reckon that the sufferings of this present time are not worthy to be compared with the glory which shall be revealed in us."

ROMANS 8:18

CHAPTER 8: HOW CAN I WORSHIP YOU IF I CANNOT TRUST YOU?

◆ ◆ ◆

Before writing this manuscript, I began reading 1st Samuel chapter 1. For those of you who are not familiar with the story, it involves a man named Elkanah, who had two wives. One was named Hannah and the other Peninnah. While Peninnah had children, Hannah was barren and had none. In those days, barrenness was considered a curse.

Elkanah was a holy man who made a pilgrimage to Shilo every year to worship God and to make sacrifices. On these pilgrimages, he took both of his wives. He gave each wife great gifts, however, to Hannah he always gave double because she had no children and was sorely vexed in her soul. Additionally, her adversary, Peninnah, took every occasion to mock Hannah, flaunting her motherhood and making Hannah cry. Can you imagine how Hannah felt? She read the word and the word said, "Ask anything in My name and you shall receive it." "For I know the thoughts that I think toward you, saith the Lord, thoughts of peace and not evil, to give you an expected end." She would prepare to make this journey to go worship God and pray for a child each year, and each year she would come back childless. However, Peninnah had a newborn every time they went to worship.

Can you imagine Hannah saying in her heart the same thing that you have quietly said in your heart: "How can I worship You if I cannot trust You?" This is the height of spiritual warfare, where Satan sits on a throne in your mind and not only lies to you but shows you some facts to back his lie up. These are not just lies, but HOT LIES! The Bible says in 1 Peter 4:12, "Beloved, think it not strange concerning the fiery trial which is to try you as though some strange thing happened to you." This is where your relationship with God is put to the test. Everything you said you believed God for at testimony time is on the altar. Every endearing name you've called God in worship is going to be tested to see if you believe it. When God tests His believers or His worshippers, He tests them for two reasons: 1) to build character and 2) to fulfill a purpose.

In Hannah's case, God already knew she was sold out, but what Hannah did not know is that God had her "on purpose." What was God's purpose? If you read 1st Samuel 1:8-15 you will see that this time that Hannah went to worship, she was extremely depressed, vexed in spirit, and almost in a crazed state. The priest, thinking she was drunk, asked her what was wrong. She shared with him that she poured her spirit out to the Lord for a male child and He didn't answer her. This time she poured out her soul. That's what God was waiting for. He heard her petition every time and purposed to answer her. But when she poured out her soul, something magnificent happened. In 1 Samuel 2:1-10, Hannah prayed a prayer that became scripture.

What's so important about that? What's so important is that 1000 years later, someone prayed a prayer very similar to her prayer. Do you know who that was? It was the mother of Jesus. In Luke 1:34, when the angel came to Mary and announced that she would have a child, Mary responded, "How could this be seeing I know no man?" Mary was having intractable difficulties trying to understand how she would have a child without having intimacy. Mary then referred back to 1 Samuel 1:2 and began to believe, and the Messiah was believed into the world.

The purpose of God was not to do evil to Hannah but to wait until she poured out her soul. When He answered her prayer, her thanks were so fervent they became part of scripture that Mary needed in order to believe Jesus into the world. Moreover, Samuel was the greatest of Elkanah's children and anointed one of the greatest prophets in biblical history.

What lesson did we learn from Hannah's experience? The lesson is that a believer should look at Hannah's resolve. That word "resolve" should be familiar to most Americans. Over the last 25 years, every time that our country has gone to war, our President has always addressed the nation to discuss the country's resolve. Merriam Webster dictionary defines resolve: "To make a definite serious decision to move forward on something with no turning back." Although Hannah was discouraged, vexed, stressed, and depressed, her resolve to go up to Shilo to worship God was not hindered. She moved forward in her twisted condition and received the promises of God despite her past futile attempts of having a male child.

Whenever you are in a position where you just want to give up, get your Bible and turn to Matthew 24:35. It says: "Heaven and earth shall pass away, but my words (promises) shall not pass away." If you walk outside and heaven and earth are still there, keep worshipping.

> Trust in the Lord with all thine heart; and lean not unto thine own understanding. In all thy ways acknowledge him, and he shall direct thy paths.
>
> PROVERBS 3:5-6

CHAPTER 9: YOU HAVE NO CLUE

◆ ◆ ◆

"Thou hast been in Eden the garden of God; every precious stone was thy covering, the sardius, topaz, and the diamond, the beryl, the onyx, and the jasper, the sapphire, the emerald, and the carbuncle, and gold: the workmanship of thy tabrets and of the pipes was prepared in thee in the day that thou hast created."

EZEKIEL 28:13

This verse is a portrait of the King of Tyre, who represents a vivid picture of Lucifer, or the devil/Satan, if you will. God even mentioned in verses 12-15 that Lucifer was the most perfect of God's creations, full of wisdom and beauty, perfect in every way until iniquity was found in him. What was the iniquity? Lucifer wanted worship. How do we know? We know by reading Isaiah 14:12-13 which says, "How art thou fallen from heaven, O Lucifer, son of the morning! How are thou cut down to the ground, which didst weaken the nations! For thou hast said in thine heart, I will ascend into heaven, I will exalt my throne above the stars of God: I will sit also upon the mount of the congregation, in the sides of the north." Satan through his illusion attempted to steal God's worship. Angels as well as humans are created beings and can offer God nothing. The only thing that an angel or human can give God is worship.

When you read the Bible, Jesus and Satan are referred to as the bright morning star. The idea of a bright morning star is a star that outshines all others. Satan, while perhaps the most beautiful creation of God and the most powerful of all the angels, was the bright morning star. While there appears to be a similarity, there is a stark difference. Satan is a created being, and his light only shines or exists to the extent that God created him. Jesus' light is self-existent, and He is the light of the world. So, whenever the devil sees that light, his sole purpose is to put it out. How does Satan put God's light out? With a lie.

Underscored below are two examples.

> *"Again, the devil taketh Jesus up into an exceeding high mountain, and sheweth him all the kingdoms of the world, and the glory of them; and saith unto him, all these things will I give thee, if thou wilt fall down and worship me. Then saith Jesus unto him, Get thee hence, Satan; for it its written, thou shalt worship the Lord they God, and him only shalt thou serve."*

MATTHEW 4:8-10

> *"Now the serpent was more subtle than any beast of the field which the LORD God had made. And he said unto the woman, Yea, hath God said, Ye shall not eat of every tree of the garden? And the woman said unto the serpent, we may eat of the fruit of the trees of the garden: but of the fruit of the tree which is in the midst of the garden, God hath said, ye shall not eat of it, neither shall ye touch it, lest ye die. And the serpent said unto the woman, Ye shall not surely die for God doth know that in the day ye eat thereof, then your eyes shall be opened, and ye shall be as gods, knowing good and evil. And when the woman saw that the tree was good for food, and that it was pleasant to the eyes, and a tree to be desired to make one wise, she took of the fruit thereof, and did eat, and gave also unto her husband with her; and he did eat."*

GENESIS 3:1-6

The question at bar here is, what tool did Satan use to get a victory, and what was used to defeat Satan? The answer is Satan used a lie to get the victory and Christ used the word of God, which is truth, to defeat him. The biggest fallacy is to mistake the innate character of Satan as a Hollywood character such as Freddy Kruger, Jason from Friday the 13th, Damien, and the like. Jesus says very simply in: John 8:41-47, "The devil is a liar and the father of lies, and there is no truth in him." Jesus then describes his purpose in John 10:10, saying, "The thief comes for one reason, to rob, kill and destroy."

What is the devil trying to steal, kill, and destroy? Your light!

"Let your light so shine before men, that they may see your good works and glorify your father who is in heaven."

MATTHEW 5:16

If Satan can cause you to believe his lie, you will not glorify God. He is not the "Boogie Man," he is a liar. When you hear a preacher say, "The devil pushed me down the steps," it's a lie. They say, "The devil punched me in the mouth," it is a lie. "The devil had sex with them," it is a lie. The devil is a spirit; he is non-corporeal, he is not a physical being, and does not have an extension in space. How he works is a mystery. While we know Satan cannot read our minds, he can influence our thoughts. He metaphysically sits on our shoulders and whispers in the ear of our minds.

We cannot explain the mind-to-mind communication, but we know it is as real as the skin on our bodies. So, we are clear through scripture that the weapons of our warfare are not physical, since this is not a physical fight. It is a spiritual fight, and Ephesians 6:10-19 tells us exactly how to prepare for its battle.

When Jesus was in a battle with Satan, He did not say, "Satan, you're evil," or "God doesn't like ugly." Instead, He did the most powerful thing a believer can do, and that was to give Satan the word of God. The only words Jesus used to Satan were: "It is written." He said it twice, and it was the only tool He used. Why did He do that? It's simple: the only way to kill a lie is to replace it with God's truth. Example: have you ever been lied to by Satan? You rebuke the lie or temptation and walk away fantasizing about the temptation, and then hours, days, or weeks later you fall into the same temptation that you rebuked. Why did you fall? You rebuked it didn't you? The reason you failed is because you need more than a "rebuke." To not detest Satan but rather to defeat Satan, you have to replace God's truth with Satan's lie and then Satan's lie dies a horrible death. Frequently believers casually throw around the phrase, "the devil is a liar" without giving serious consideration to the power and depth of his lies to believers as well as non-believing humanity. His ostensible purpose is to stop you from worshipping God. This is how he operates in Adam and Eve's defeat. The first thing the devil did was to replace God's truth with his lie: "Hath He said ye shall not eat of every tree of the Garden?" He first causes doubt, then he discourages, lastly, he replaces God's truth with his lie. "And the serpent said to the woman, you shall not surely die." Wow, Satan opened deaths door with a lie.

Now to the worshipper who is going through a trial, season, etc., the reason you are passing through it is because God values and honors your worship. The enemy knows it, understands, and wants to steal your worship so that he can kill it and destroy it. Come out of that funk. Put on the full armor of God as defined in Ephesians 6:10-19 and position yourself to receive your breakthrough.

> "Be sober, be vigilant; because your adversary the devil,
> as a roaring lion, walketh about, seeking whom he may devour."

> 1 PETER 5:8

CHAPTER 10: TWO DEAD
BATTERIES CANNOT START A CAR

◆ ◆ ◆

Recently my neighbor was attempting to start his car one cold morning, only to find out that his battery had died. Another neighbor tried to offer assistance, and low and behold, his battery cells were very low and near dead itself. I had just purchased a new battery for my car about a month before, so I offered my assistance. When I connected the cables, the car started right up.

In the prior chapter, we talked about how the enemy attempts to stop your worship. One good way is to paralyze your worship. The scripture says that God inhabits the place where He is praised and worshipped. If there is no one there to worship Him, He cannot perform. If He cannot perform, then your situation is like two dead batteries. When Jesus was in Nazareth, He did no miracles. Why not? Because there was no belief. When He performed miracles, He was with His disciples, particularly Peter, James, and John. He would call these three of the twelve to witness His miracles. Why did He leave the others? Was Christ prejudiced, arrogant, conceited? No, none of the above. He just knew that two dead batteries cannot start a car.

I would like to share an extraordinarily strong Bible verse whose origins is in Luke 18:35-43: "And it came to pass, that as He was come nigh unto Jericho, a certain blind man sat by the wayside begging: And hearing the multitude pass by, he asked what it meant. And they told him, that Jesus of Nazareth passeth by. And he cried saying, Jesus, thou Son of David have mercy on me. And they which went before rebuked him, that he should hold his peace, but he cried so much the more, Thou Son of David have mercy on me. And Jesus stood, and commanded him to be brought to him: And when he was come near, he asked him, Saying, what wilt thou that I shall do unto thee? And he said Lord, that I may receive my sight. And Jesus said unto him, Receive thy sight: Thy faith hath saved thee. And immediately he received his sight, and followed him, glorifying God: And all the people, when they saw it, gave praise unto God."

Wow, here is a man who is not only blind but poor. He hears that Jesus is passing by, and at the point of knowing it is Jesus, on cue he began to worship. When he called Jesus, Son of David, that was tantamount to calling Him God in the flesh, because the Messiah would come from the genealogy of David. As Jesus was walking there was a multitude following Him, which I believe would have made it difficult for Him to hear anyone while the people were constantly telling blind Bartimaeus to be quiet, but he refused, shouting louder every time, shouting, "Jesus, Son of David." Then suddenly, out of at least 5000 people, Jesus commands Bartimaeus to come to Him. Why did Jesus do that? Because He heard worship. He saw faith through public worship. He heard the scream, and as the scream got louder, He heard in it His name, Jesus, Son of David. That is what Jesus came to reveal to the Jews. But out of all the Jews thronging Him, only one yelled out and worshipped Him. The result, blind Bartimaeus received his sight. I wonder what would have happened if he would have kept his mouth shut.

But as it is written, Eye hath not seen, nor ear heard, neither have entered into the heart of man, the things which God hath prepared for them that love him.

1 CORINTHIANS 2:9

CHAPTER 11: WHY DID YOU EVEN CALL ME? (GOING IN ON GOD)

◆ ◆ ◆

And Moses returned unto the Lord, and said, Lord, wherefore hast thou so evil entreated this people? Why is it that thou hast sent me? For since I came to Pharaoh to speak in thy name, he hath done evil to this people; neither hast thou delivered thy people at all.

EXODUS 5:22-23

Wow! The children of Israel were in bondage for approximately 430 years. God sent the children a deliverer named Moses. Moses exchanged his lifestyle of a wealthy, famous, Egyptian architect and lord in Pharaoh's house to become a Hebrew slave that was exiled. During Moses' transition, he met with God. Just like Moses, before anyone can meet with God they have to be taken to a low place. In Pharaoh's house, it was difficult for Moses to hear the voice of God. God's voice is drowned out when you have money, women, talent, high self-esteem, worldly favor, etc. When Moses killed the Egyptian and was exiled to the wilderness, He met God face to face. In the wilderness there was lack. Lack is an immensely powerful word and a spiritual tool that both the devil and God use. In the wilderness, Moses lacked reputation, money, self-esteem, and most of all PRIDE. When all of that was lost, God revealed Himself.

When God revealed Himself, Moses asked God a deep question: "When I come to the children of Israel and say to them, the God of your fathers has sent me to you and they shall say to me, what is His name? What shall I say to them?" God said to Moses, "I AM THAT I AM." Wow! Most theologians believe that this name means "the self-existent one" or "I will be what I will be." They all may be correct. I believe that during the discourse between Moses and God, He stated his name was I AM THAT I AM because He couldn't think of a name that could properly identify His majesty and glory.

Like you and I, when Moses met God, he viewed Him from a certain perspective that I have coined as "abracadabra." Abracadabra is a Hebrew/Aramaic word that means, "I will create right away." Moses must have said within himself, "This isn't going to be too difficult because THE GREAT I AM has sent me. It is just a matter of going to Pharaoh and giving him God's instructions, and then I am out of there." Not!

When God calls His people, He calls them through faith. Faith, however, is worthless unless it is challenged or tested. In Exodus chapter 5, Moses went to the people expecting "abracadabra." Instead, their faith was put on trial. While on trial, in its appearance, the word of God looked void. When Moses consistently declared who God was and what He could do, things got progressively worse. Moses did something that you (the reader and worshipper) are scared to do: he went in on God. Moses told God, "for since I came to speak to Pharaoh in your name, things have gotten worse, neither have you delivered at all." To be brutally honest, Moses told God He failed.

Of course, the story doesn't end there. In Exodus 6:1, God responds to Moses' comment:

> Then the Lord said unto Moses, now shalt thou see what I will do to Pharaoh: For with a strong hand shall he let them go, and with a strong hand shall he drive them out of his land.

EXODUS 6:1

When you read the rest of the story in Exodus, things became so deep for Pharaoh that he asked Moses to intercede and pray to God for him. At the very end, the children of Israel left Egypt and went into a land that God gave them, along with the possessions of the Egyptians.

Approximately six years ago I attended a church service in New York. A woman came to the service for healing. I observed that she had a rare skin condition, and the more the pastor prayed for her, the worse her condition became. When I shook the pastor's hand after the service, I could see discouragement in his eyes. The following week, the same lady attended the testimony services and stated that her condition worsened to a new level in that her skin was peeling off of her body. In frustration, the pastor said, "I don't know what God is doing. I know His word is true, however, your situation has led me to question my calling. All that I can tell you to do now is worship Him." Three weeks passed and the woman was a no-show at the weekly services. On the fourth Sunday, she not only attended services but she lit the sanctuary up with her testimony. She said, just like Moses, she went in on God. She told God she didn't believe Him and that she didn't trust Him, but all that she had left was to worship Him. The following day she reported skin growth that occurred for the next several days. Through her worship, she was completely healed. Her doctors had no explanation, and deemed it a medical phenomenon. I call it a miracle.

There are going to be times when you question why God even called you, or what His purpose is for your life. You question what He is doing when you pray and hope that this is when faith trumps condition.

God's purpose for a worshipper is to bring them to an expected end. What the end will be, when will it be, I don't know. What I do know is, it will be.

> He staggered not at the promise of God through unbelief;
> but was strong in faith, giving glory to God.
>
> ROMANS 8:20

CHAPTER 12: OH NO, YOU DIDN'T!

◆ ◆ ◆

And when he came to the den he cried with a lamentable voice, "unto Daniel" and the King spoke and said to Daniel, "O Daniel servant of the living God, is thy God, whom you worship continually able to deliver thee from the lions."

DANIEL 6:20

D aniel was a young man who, at the age of 16, was forced into slavery in a strange land. He became God's prophetic mouthpiece to the Jews in slavery as well as to the Gentiles who held them captive. Sinners who worshipped idols described Daniel as a man who had the spirit of a Holy God, who walked in excellence, interpreted dreams, and worshipped God continually.

One day, a group of despisers got together to find fault with Daniel since he had favor with God and the king. They couldn't find fault, so they assembled themselves and persuaded the king to sign a decree that stated that if anyone petitions the king or God for 30 days they would be thrown into the lion's den as punishment. Later that day according to Daniel's custom, he faced the East to pray three times a day. He was observed praying and worshipping, was taken into custody, and against the king's will, was thrown into the lions' den.

I can only imagine Daniel saying, "Oh no, he didn't!" In a worshipper's life, there are times while serving God that he observes the unrighteous prosper and says in his heart, "Oh no, he didn't!" How could God allow His holy, righteous servant Daniel, who brought Him glory continuously, to be sitting in the lions' den after worshipping Him?

God cautions the worshipper in Psalms 37: "Fret not because of evildoers, neither be thou envious of workers of iniquity, for they soon will be cut down like the grass and wither like the green herb." While we understand what God said and we know His word is true, sometimes it becomes very difficult to worship God and yet sit and watch the wicked prosper. You will have experiences in the kingdom of God that the more carnal a church is, the more it seems to prosper, and if you're not careful, it can affect your worship. For instance, you work two jobs, live paycheck to paycheck, and you worship God continually. When it comes time for vacation, the neighbors are going to the Bahamas and you are going to "Porchville" – your front porch. On Sunday through worship, you usher in the spirit of God, then you have a believer who never honors God in their ways stand up and testify that one of their sons has just graduated from the police academy and the other son is on his way to law school. One of your children, on the other hand, is in jail while your daughter is pole dancing at the Purple Orchid Strip Club.

You begin to doubt the sovereignty of God, and if you are not careful, motivation starts to leave your worship. This is why the enemy sits on your shoulder and whispers in the ear of your mind, "Look at that, can you believe that?" You respond in your heart, "Oh no, you didn't!"

The devil knows what worship is and the effects it has on the spirit of God. If he can get you to concentrate on others and whisper in the ear of your mind, eventually he is going to steal that worship.

The Bible says, "rest in the Lord and wait patiently for him. Fret not thyself of him who prospereth in this way, because of the men who bringeth wicked devices to pass." Three key words in this verse from Psalms 37 are "rest" and " wait patiently." When Daniel was thrown into the lions' den, I find it hard to believe that his faith wasn't challenged with some tough questions: "C'mon God, why me, why not him or her? I did everything you asked me continually."

While I was pondering the story, as well as my own and the story of Tim Tebow, an athlete who boldly worshipped God even though his career failed, I thought about other athletes such as Lebron James and Tom Brady, who have major success without even the mention of the God who gave them the physical ability and gifts to do the things they do. I gingerly began to question God about His ways, His promises, and the manifestation in worshippers. Suddenly, the Holy Spirit bore witness on January 28, 2015, at approximately 11:45 am. I heard His voice say: "Because I need worship." I knew it was God because I had experienced His physical voice at least three other times during my ministry, so it was familiar to me. There was something very different about the way God spoke this time. It wasn't very authoritative or bold but was very meek and sheepish, and as He said it, it appeared that He was crying. I immediately went into my imagination and pictured God saying over and over again, "I need worship." He then began to speak out of the whirlwind in a tearful voice saying, "The reason Daniel was put into the lions' den is because I needed worship."

I recently observed something on my job, as well as all over the kingdom, where the wicked appeared to prosper and the righteous (worshippers) appeared to fail. Approximately three years ago I met a woman on my job named April Barfield. At first blush, she appeared to be religious because every word she uttered was "amen," "praise the Lord," and "hallelujah." I began to wonder if she knew any other words. If you went on her Facebook page you would see "Glory to God"; her Twitter page, "Praise the Lord"; Instagram, "Hallelujah." During my observation of her, it was consistent that everywhere her foot landed, she lifted up the name of Jesus and she lived Christ. On the same unit, there was another woman who constantly quipped, "Hallelujah," "Glory to God," and "Jesus loves you," however, she lived differently from her testimony. Now what was telling is that both received different results. The worshipper worked with integrity and lived for God, but her work hours were always shortened, she was accused falsely of various things, her car was repossessed, and she had other financial challenges at home. The other believer who walked around preaching Christ but lived like Jezebel, always involved in scandals that were swept under the rug, received so many hours she had to give some of them away. She purchased a brand-new car and a new house in an upscale neighborhood.

One day on my way to work, I noticed the worshipper coming from afar, shaking her head. As I approached her, I asked her what was wrong. She briskly said, "Praise the Lord, I just don't get it." Due to her frustration and our only crossing paths from time to time, I wasn't able to get to her meaning of, "I just don't get it." However, if I was a betting man and I had $1000 to wager, I'd bet $999 that "I just don't get it" meant, "Lord I worship you day and night, on social media, on my job, while I'm shopping, driving, even in my sleep, and this is how you treat me? This one over there preaches your name but lives like the abstract devil, cusses, fornicates, gossips, steals, lies, and cheats, you name it, she does it. Is this sowing and reaping, is this how you treat the object of your worship?"

"The reason Hezekiah was sick is because I needed worship. The reason Jehoshaphat had three armies come against him is because I needed worship. The reason I destroyed the whole earth and saved only Noah and his family is because I needed worship. The reason Tim Tebow didn't go to the Superbowl but Tom Brady did is because Tebow worships me, Brady does not. If Tebow got the glamor, glitz, and pride of life he would forget ME, and I wouldn't get my worship."

As God's voice started to quiet, I began to ponder and concluded with, every person He mentioned went through something but yet became victorious. Worship has to be based on a "come what may" mindset because it is the mindset that illustrates you do it out of love. 1 Corinthians 13:7 gives a description of what love is: "Love bears all things, believes all things, endures all things." How can the devil attempt to steal your worship? With a mindset like that, He has nothing to tempt you with.

In conclusion, the real response to God is "Yes, He did." Yes, He did send His only begotten Son to pay for your sins. Yes, He did stop that bullet from coming around the corner and hitting your son. Yes, He did stop cancer when it was heading in your direction. Yes, He did provide shelter for you when you were penniless. Yes, He did keep you when you didn't want to be kept. Yes, He did make a way out of no way. Yes, He did leave this earth to go prepare a place for you where there is no more death, pain, or tears. Yes, He did it all so come what may, He deserves worship!

Worship the LORD with gladness, come before Him with joyful songs.

PSALMS 100:2

CHAPTER 13: STOP THE MUSIC

◆ ◆ ◆

By the waters of Babylon, there we sat down, yea, we wept, when we remembered Zion. We hanged our harps upon the willows in the midst thereof. For there they that carried us away captive required of us a song; and they that wasted us required of us mirth, saying, Sing us one of the songs of Zion. How long shall we sing the LORD's song in a strange land?

PSALMS 137:1-4

This is a true story about the children of Israel (or the first church) when they were taken from their home into captivity or slavery in a strange land. Home for a Jew was quite different in those days. In the Jewish home, they served their own God, ate kosher meals, and the land was flowing with milk and honey, meaning everyone had their means of making money. There was no poverty, no strife, and it was basically like heaven on earth.

A petition was set by the oppressors (or the devil) against the Jews for them to sing them a song of Zion. What was meant when the oppressor said sing us a song of Zion is, sing us one of those spiritual victory songs like the one in Exodus 15:1. Then Moses and the children of Israel sang this song: "I will sing to the Lord for He has triumphed gloriously, the horse and the rider He has thrown into the sea." The oppressors were taunting the believers, and the believers' response was, "How can we sing the Lord's song in a strange place?" Strange places in those days meant taking them from all of God's promises in Israel. A strange place today is quite the same, but it is a spiritual change, not a geographical one. "How can I sing the Lord's song when I testified in church and on my job that the Lord blessed me with a new car last year and this year the repo man took my car while I was at work, in front of my co-workers? How can I sing the Lord's song when six months ago I was diagnosed with stage I cancer? I confessed that God was a healer and the cancer was gone, only to be diagnosed again with stage III cancer. How can I sing the Lord's song when I post a picture of my dream house on Facebook, give God all the glory for giving it to me, and then two years later I'm in foreclosure? How can I sing the Lord's song when I testified that my daughter had been delivered from crack last year and on my way from church, I saw her prostituting to earn money for crack?" How can you sing the Lord's song when you are doing everything positive that you can while the disobedient, carnal believer has all your visions, hopes, and prayers active in their lives and you don't have enough to cover your tithes?

So the question is, "Lord I love you, I honor you, I give you glory, and I lift you up, but how do I sing the Lord's song in a strange place?"

One of God's favorite words is "if" and in Psalms 137:5-6 He employs those words: "If I forget thee, O Jerusalem let my right hand forget her skill. If I do not remember thee, let my tongue cleave to the roof of my mouth If I prefer not Jerusalem above my chief joy."

The Bible was written to the Jews for the world. When you read this verse, take out "Jerusalem" and put your name in its place and then read it reciting your name, because God is not just speaking to the Jews – He is speaking to the believers.

Now when you read the scripture of promise for all it is worth, it will reveal to you, the worshipper, that God is saying, "If I don't answer your prayer let my right hand forget her skill (the right hand of God is power), let my tongue cleave to the roof of my mouth." God speaks things into existence with the tongue. So what God is essentially saying (and I confirmed this with a nurse from the University of Pennsylvania hospital) is, "If I don't answer your prayer (Cherese, Arnold, Sarah, Tom, Pam, Malik, Constance, Maria), let me have a stroke." Medically speaking, when your hand loses function and your tongue cleaves to the roof of your mouth you are in stroke mode. So instead of stopping the music, the attitude should be let the music play. It is very difficult to serve God in adverse situations or a strange place when your mind is concentrated on your issues. This is where the enemy is at his best paralyzing, muzzling, and stifling your worship. He used to be God's chief worshipper, and nobody knows better than Lucifer how to entreat God's presence; likewise, nobody knows better how to keep the presence of God afar.

If you've ever studied quantum physics, you will see that clapping, singing, and loud noises shift the atmosphere. When you begin worshipping a Holy God, in order for His presence to come in there must be a shift in the atmosphere, and only worship shifts the atmosphere. When there is no worship the atmosphere stays the same, and so does your crisis.

In order for you to continue singing the Lord's song in that condition, you must do two things. First, you must develop a vision: "If there is no vision the people perish." YOUR BODY CAN NOT GO WHERE YOUR MIND HASN'T BEEN TO FIRST. Second, you must surround yourself with people who believe in your vision, understand reality, and believe God. When the Ark of the Covenant came to Israel, as the Bible says in 2 Samuel Chapter 6, David danced with all his heart, but Saul's daughter, Michal, despised David for worshipping God in that manner. David knew something about the presence of God and worship. David was told by Saul's daughter that he embarrassed Israel by the way he worshipped God. David's response was, if you think that was something wait till the next worship. I am going to be even more indignant than that. David was clear on how to worship God and the result of worship was also clear. Michal died childless, while David died rich, peaceful, and his son, Solomon, took over where he left off.

Do not stop singing, I know what it looks like to let the music play.

It is a good thing to give thanks unto the LORD, and to sing praises unto thy name, O most High.

PSALMS 92:1

CHAPTER 14: FROM A HARD PLACE TO WORSHIP

◆ ◆ ◆

And Jacob rose early in the morning and took the stone that he had put for his pillows, and set it up for a pillar, and poured oil upon the top of it. And he called the name of that place Beth-el: But the name of the city was called Luz at the first.

GENESIS 28:18-19

When reading the Bible, in the book of Genesis you will observe that Jacob, from birth, was associated with strife, struggles, and difficulties that always placed him in what I coin as a "hard place." A hard place is a dilemma, a tight spot, a hard decision, a lose-lose situation, a place where you can't make up your mind. Frequently in the life of a worshipper, we find ourselves in these situations. In Genesis chapter 28, God made Jacob some promises that staggered the human imagination. Jacob was in a hard place as opposed to the promises of Almighty God. What is telling is, although Jacob was in a hard place, that place became his place of worship. When Jacob anointed the hard place (the stone), he set it as a place of worship (the pillar).

Whenever God allows tribulation, strife, or hard times to come into your life, it's designed to drive you into worship. In the book of Matthew 8:1-2 it says, "And behold there came a leper and worshipped Him." In Matthew 9:18 it says, "While He spoke behold there was a certain ruler and worshipped Him saying my daughter is dead." In the book of John 9:38, the blind man that Jesus gave sight to says, "And he said, Lord, I believe, and he worshipped Him."

Leprosy, blindness, and death are all extremely loathsome situations that can cause you to be in what is called a hard place. A hard place by nature causes a human to seek God for the impossible. This is the time when the Almighty gets the chance to glorify Himself by saving you from the hard place. In turn, you reciprocate by worshipping Him. You reciprocate by reminding Him of who He is, where you were, what would have happened if He didn't show up, how you felt about what He did, and that He can do a repeat performance. This is why scripture says in Romans 8:28, "And we know all things work together for the good..." Your hard place has a purpose. If you've never been sick, you would never know Him as a healer. If you've never experienced lack, you would never know He is a provider. If you never had unrest in your life, you would never know He is the God of peace. So, your hard place is not by coincidence, it is by design. God didn't put it there, but He always uses the opportunity for you to get to know Him. If you know Him, He wants to reveal Himself in another way that will bless you. The promising thing is, He has to bless you or He won't get what He came there for, and that is worship.

Worship the Lord in the splendor of His holiness.

PSALM 29:2

51

CHAPTER 15: HOW CAN I WORSHIP MY SLAVE MASTER'S GOD?

◆ ◆ ◆

When you look for me with all your heart you will find me.

JEREMIAH 29:13

Recently I was chatting with a friend of mine named Curtis Tate, whom I coin as a "humble intellectual." He shared with me that a woman once shared a random post on social media showing Ronald McDonald sitting in the pew of a church, signaling to the audience that one would have to be a clown to become a Christian. As alarming and ghastly as the woman's post was, to a great many people, specifically people of color, it appeared to be logical.

The biggest problem that African, Afro Americans, and people of color have with the Bible is the IMAGERY of all the prophets and Jesus being Caucasian. The danger with IMAGERY is that it shapes the mind to relate that image to any image, whether evil or good, that the individual chooses and associates that image with God. Example: If I am a person of color and for all of my life I have only observed the IMAGERY of Jesus Christ as Caucasian, in my subjective mind (a mind that lacks critical thinking) I would shape the nature and character of God as a Klansman or white police officer who kills an unarmed Black male or female. Then without objective thinking, I would reject the Bible based on the image and not the unadulterated facts of the person of Jesus the Christ.

QUESTIONS THEN ARISE LIKE, "HOW CAN YOU WORSHIP YOUR SLAVE MASTER'S GOD?"

To answer this theory or question, one must first question the question to even see if the question is valid. Instead of perception, one must go to the cold hard facts. The only place to get the facts is from the one you indicted, and that is the God of the Judeo-Christian faith who was and is revealed in The Holy Bible.

Enumerated below are four scriptures out of hundreds that will validate that this theory is invalid or just pure fallacious thinking.

"Behold I am the God of all flesh." (All Humans)

JEREMIAH 32:27

"For God so loved the world (Blacks) that he gave His only begotten son that whosoever (Blacks) will not perish but have eternal existence."

JOHN 3:16

"We trust in the living God who is the SAVIOR of all men (Blacks included)."

1ST TIM 4:10

"If I am lifted up, I will draw all men (Black men) to myself."

JOHN 12:32

When a person, whether Caucasian, Black, Hispanic, Asian, Indian, Aborigine, or any human, reads scripture they develop a sense of personal intimacy with God, because apart from IMAGERY the scriptures are talking expressly to mankind in a loving, caring, affectionate, and compassionate manner about the issues of life.

Concerning slavery, here is the Judeo-Christian God attitude towards it:

Follow peace with all men or without no man will see God.

HEBREWS 12:14

This is the commandment that we have from God that he who loves God must love his brother.

1ST JOHN 4:21

For whoremongers, liars and Men stealers (slave catchers) will not see the Kingdom of God.

1ST TIMOTHY 1:10

So, if we are committed to truth, one can see that God is Sovereign. He does not participate in race, political parties, human bondage, and the like, nor does He participate in color. The scripture is clear in Acts 17:29, "For as much as we are the offspring of God, we ought not to think that His nature and character are anything like gold, silver, stone, or man's graven art. And the times of this ignorance God winked at it in times past but causing all men to repent today." Some may say, wasn't Jesus Black according to the book of Revelations 1:8-9 where it said, "Jesus had hair like wool and His skin like burnt brass"? The answer is a resounding no! That's counter racism in which God transcends or does not participate in that realm of thinking.

When the Apostle John was describing Christ, he was not describing the Christ that walked the earth who came as a lamb to serve; rather, he was describing the future Christ who is coming as a LION to judge. When the scripture speaks of white hair like wool from ancient days, it is talking about eternity. When it mentions feet like burnt brass, burnt brass symbolizes judgment. So, at its taproot, God was very wise to hide Jesus' complexion because it would have been an excellent platform for racism. As a theology teacher, I study all religions and have very good loving relationships with people of all faiths, especially Islam.

One of the fastest-growing religions on Earth is Islam. One of the reasons is because, and I want you to think about this carefully, THERE ARE NO IMAGES OF MUHAMMAD. What's puzzling is that it is mostly Muslims of color who are the ones that frequently ask the question, "How can you worship your slave master's God?" The reason for the question is because of the volatile relationships of Whites versus Blacks throughout history. When I study Islamic history, one thing I can say is they faithfully recorded their history even if it seemed unseemly. One would wonder how Blacks or people of color can be conspicuously silent when reading verses like this from the Hadith (Muslim Holy Book):

I heard the apostle say whoever wants to see Satan should look at Nabtal. He was a Black man with long flowing hair, inflamed eyes, and dark ruddy cheeks.

ISHAG:243

We know that the Zanj (blacks) are the least intelligent and the least discerning of Mankind.

AL-SAHIZ (781-869AD)

Blacks are ugly and mis-happened because they live in a hot country.

IBN QUTAYBAH (828-889AD)

Blacks are people by their very nature are slaves.

IBN SINA (980-1037AD)

The negro nation as a rule is submissive to slavery because the Negros have little that is essential to humans and have attributes that are quite similar to those of dumb animals.

IBN KHALDUN (1332-1406 AD)

As we have stated, this is not a knock on the precious souls of the kingdom of Islam, rather it's a depiction to show how dangerous IMAGERY can be portrayed. When you begin looking at movies such as Roots, Amistad, or Mississippi Burning, if a person is not careful or objective (asks questions), one could hold a Holy God accountable for what a group of evil, diabolical Caucasians did to African American people during slavery.

It is clear that the Bible predates African slavery by 1500 years, and it forewarns all men to live in peace and commands all races and nationalities to love one another. Because you see empirical evidence that God condemns slavery and racism, one should never attempt to use slavery and racism as a scapegoat not to worship God if they are committed to truth.

In conclusion, the slave master or Caucasians do not have exclusive rights to God, and if they were in a proper relationship with God, African slavery would have never existed. One of the main reasons it doesn't exist today in America is that many have woken up to the sobering Biblical truths that ALL people are created by God with innate equality.

> And God hath made from One Blood all nations of men for to live on the face of the Earth and has determined the times before appointed and the boundaries of where they will live.

> ACTS 17:26

CHAPTER 16: OR SHOULD I
LOOK FOR ANOTHER?

◆ ◆ ◆

*The next day John seeth Jesus coming unto him, and saith, behold
the Lamb of God, which taketh away the sin of the world. This is he
of whom I said, after me cometh a man which is preferred before
me: For he was before me. And I knew him not: but that he should
be made manifest to Israel, therefore am I come baptizing with
water. And John bare record, saying, I saw the Spirit descending
from heaven like a dove, and it abode upon him. And I knew him
not: But he that sent me to baptize with water, the same said unto
me, upon whom thou shalt see the Spirit descending, and remain-
ing on him, the same is he which baptizeth with the Holy Ghost.
And I saw, and bare record that this is the Son of God.*

JOHN 1:29-34

Israel was awaiting its Messiah for approximately 2000 years.
At this announcement, there was a prophecy in the book of
Isaiah about a forerunner of the Messiah that would come in
the spirit of Elijah. He would make the path straight and identify
exactly who the Messiah would be. John the Baptist was the forerunner and my God, did he give Jesus one heck of an introduction.

John the Baptist was a man full of faith, who had a heart for
God and spoke boldly about the things of God. One day John rebuked a Jewish leader named Herod for having an adulterous relationship. This ultimately landed John in jail. At some point while
in jail, he asked a question that just about every believer has
asked God. John, however, said it openly to his disciples when he
asked: "Go ask Jesus is He the Christ or should we look for another
one?"

When a human is conceived in the mind of God, he or she is actualized through a series of tests. Before a human is conceived, he must plod through 60 million cells to become a human. From the time it is in the womb to its last day breathing on earth, a human will be tested. And when you begin to believe God, your faith, like your life, will be tested. Faith that is challenged by some tough questions, situations, etc., becomes a sounder faith in the end.

If you are brutally honest and committed to the truth, this question haunts you: "Are you the Christ or do we look for another?" There's an old saying, "talk is cheap," and I believe the Almighty agrees with this saying. If you read scripture such as John 14:14 which says, "If you ask anything in my name I will do it," and you confess in the congregation that you believe what God said, you go on Facebook and Twitter to confess it also, but when something goes against your thinking, timing, or your hope, the question pops into your mind, "Go ask Jesus is He the Christ or should we look for another?"

When God asks a believer to believe in Him, He doesn't ask them to believe just by faith; rather, he asks a person to believe by faith based on facts. That is what separates all other religions from the Judeo-Christian faith. All other religions claim something but they never back it up by facts. Example: Buddha claimed to be the father of enlightenment, Confucius claimed to be the father of wisdom, and Mohammed claimed to be the seal of the prophets. Jesus claimed something vastly different. He claimed to be God and backed it up by the immutable fact of the RESURRECTION.

When John's faith faltered while he was in prison, he told his disciples to go ask Jesus if He was the ONE. When Jesus was confronted with this question, His response was devastating as well as revelatory: "Go and show John again those things which you do hear and see: The blind receive their sight, the lame walk, the lepers are cleansed, the deaf hear, the dead are raised, and the gospel preached to the poor. And blessed is he, whosoever shall not be offended in me."

Let me see if I can paraphrase Jesus' statement to John's disciples. I think Jesus was saying: "Go tell John when he reads the book of Isaiah, it prophesied of the Spirit coming down on the Messiah and it came on ME in the Jordan river. He confessed that I was the Son of God, that was ME. Tell John when I gave the blind man His sight in John chapter 9, that I'm still doing it. Tell John those ten lepers in Luke 17 that I healed and only one came back to thank ME, I'm still doing it. Tell John everything that the prophet Isaiah said about the Messiah 700 years ago is fulfilled in ME today. Tell John I am still everything he said I was in John chapter 1 and because his condition changed doesn't equate that God changed."

When God reveals Himself in the Bible to various prophets, He always gives a sign or wonder to substantiate who He was. With Moses, He gave him a staff and wrought miracles through them. With Elijah, He licked up the sacrifice. With David, He saved him from the lion, tiger, and a bear. When Jesus responded to John's question, he said something very telling: "Go tell John again." Why did Jesus say "again?" The reason He said "again" is that when you are passing through a faith trial, to pass through it you may need to remember or recall God's last acts, to believe Him for the trial that's in front of you. That is why in Romans 10:17 it says, "faith comes by hearing." You must hear the word of God and recall his last acts to jump-start, empower, quicken, and ignite your faith. John began meditating on his present condition and lost sight of the facts that were revealed to him face to face.

There are times in a believer's life that, no matter how mature they are, it could be, Jakes, Dollar, Graham, etc., that little voice comes and says, "Are you the Christ or should we look for another?" This is the time where you prove your faith and your response should go something like this:

> Although the fig tree shall not blossom, neither shall fruit be in the vines; the labour of the olive shall fail, and the fields shall yield no meat; the flock shall be cut off from the fold, and there shall be no herd in the stalls: Yet I will rejoice in the LORD, I will joy in the God of my salvation. The LORD God is my strength, and he will make my feet like hinds' feet, and he will make me to walk upon mine high

places. To the chief singer on my stringed instruments.

HABAKKUK 3:17-19

What the psalmist is saying is things are ugly and all of my confessions about God, all my testimonies about my visions, have appeared to have failed, but I still trust God because if I continue to worship, to stand, to be faithful, He will–not may, not might– He will cause me to possess every vision and prayer that I trusted Him for.

In conclusion, you don't have to look for another because in all truth, there is no other one. If you can worship Him despite your condition, you will see the glory of God.

I, even I, am the LORD; and beside me there is no saviour.

ISAIAH 43:11

Who hath wrought and done it, calling the generations from the beginning? I the LORD, the first, and with the last; I am He.

ISAIAH 41:4

CHAPTER 17: PRAY FOR ME, YES; BUT WHO'S GOING TO WORSHIP HIM?

◆ ◆ ◆

On the way to Jerusalem, He was passing along between Samaria and Galilee. And as He entered a village, He was met by ten lepers, who stood at a distance and lifted up their voices saying: "Jesus, Master, Have mercy on us." When He saw them, He said to them, Go shew yourselves unto the priests. And it came to pass, that as they went, they were cleansed. Then one of them when he saw that he was healed, turned back, and with a loud voice glorified God, and fell on his face at his feet, giving Him thanks: and he was a Samaritan. And Jesus answering said: "Were there not ten cleansed? But where are the nine? They are not found that returned to give glory to God, save this stranger. And He said to him, "Arise, go thy way: thy faith hath made thee whole.

LUKE 17:11

Leprosy is a disease of the skin that causes numbness of the limbs and incurable sores. In Biblical times, leprosy was seen as a curse or a possession of one's body or spirit. A leper in those days was excommunicated to what was called a leper colony where they didn't socialize with normal humans, only with people who had the disease themselves. To short circuit my import, life for a leper was living hell day and night.

When the lepers encountered Jesus, like most people today, they implored Him for healing. But what was telling was, only one came back to thank Him and worship Him – and that person was a foreigner or a non-church going person.

Recently while working the 3 pm to 11 pm shift, I encountered a woman with a serious problem. She was a woman addicted to drugs. Before she came into the program, she shared a testimony that she had stolen a large sum of money from her aunt who raised her. Her aunt was near death and because of it, guilt was eating this woman alive. One day during her tribulation, she struck up a conversation with me about God, knowing that my craft is theology. At my primary job, I am considered deeply knowledgeable about all religions. I am very mindful that religion is sacred, so I tenderly had a conversation about the differences in Islam and Christianity, which is like the distance between east and west. She confessed that she was Muslim and admitted knowing nothing about the religion or how to pray. Because I knew that she was grieved and not looking for God but looking for religion, I prayed that God would press her tribulation to the point that she would cry out for Christ.

Two days later, on a Tuesday around 3:30 pm, God answered my prayer. I walked on to the unit and observed this Muslim woman crying in the group saying, "Oh my God, oh my God, Jesus help me!" The clients informed me that her relatives wanted to kill her and blamed her for her aunt's medical condition. I went over to console her, looked her dead in her eyes and said: "You must confront your fears." She looked at me peculiarly as if to question, how?

I took her into my office and asked if I could pray for her. She replied, "You must have read my mind." I began to pray and asked God according to Proverbs 21:1 would He move by His Spirit to change the hearts of her family, and to prove to the client that He is God and God alone, and only He is worthy of worship. Moments later after praying, I permitted her the use of the office phone and told her to call her aunt. She was very hesitant and distraught. I told her to just believe. She dialed the phone and her cousin answered. I heard an excited scream and a big smile appeared on the client's face. As I left the room, I could see her crying tears of joy. I came back into my office and just stared at her. She had the biggest Kool-Aid smile on her face. She gave me a huge embrace and said it felt like the weight of the world had been lifted off of her shoulders. She said that the relative who had threatened to kill her said that within the last half an hour, he began to think about her and pray that God would have her communicate with the family because the aunt was asking about her. She said that was God answering her prayer.

Two hours later a group meeting was facilitated, and in front of at least 200 people in the audience, the client stood up and said: "Allah, the God of the Quran, answered her prayers." I almost fell out of my chair.

God by His very nature commands worship. When Jesus made His triumphal entry into Jerusalem during the Passover, the people were thronging Him and shouting: "Hosanna, Hosanna!" The Jewish priest shouted to Jesus: "Jesus, make the people be quiet!" Jesus replied: "If these be quiet the rocks will cry out." While that appeared to be a sarcastic rebut, I believe that it is 100% true. I believe that if the true glory of God were ever revealed on earth, the entire earth would explode. God by His very existence causes creation to worship HIM. And when He performs an act, and that miracle is attributed to another source, then the Spirit of God is naturally grieved.

The next time someone asks you to pray, fast, intercede, or lay before the Lord for them, ask them this very telling and convicting question: "Who is going to worship Him?"

"That no flesh should glory in his presence."

1ST CORINTHIANS 1:29

CHAPTER 18: STRANGE

◆ ◆ ◆

And Nadab and Abihu the sons of Aaron, took either of them his censer, and put fire therein, and put incense thereon, and offered strange fire before the Lord, which He commanded them not. And there went out fire from the Lord and devoured them, and they died before the LORD.

LEVITICUS 10:1-2

If you read the book of Leviticus chapter 1, according to which translation you have, it always starts with "Now" or "And." The question at bar is now what, and what. Leviticus is God's guidebook for His newly redeemed people showing them how to worship Him. When a person worships God, he must worship God according to the way God instructs him to worship, not how man feels in his mind.

Aaron's sons came to the altar to worship God and gave a holy God strange fire. What was this strange fire? Scripture does not explain what this strange fire was, but it certainly shows how God felt about it. God then told Moses to tell Aaron, "When the people approach ME, regard ME as Holy. In other words, give ME what I ask for and not what you think I want. I ask for what I want and not what you think I want." Most humans, when it comes to worshipping God, want to worship Him according to their thinking and that is wrong. In the Catholic church, Mary is worshipped, but God is crystal clear in the scriptures that Jesus is to be worshipped alone.

"And when they had come into the house, they saw the young child with Mary his mother, and fell down, and worshipped Him...."

MATTHEW 2:11

CHAPTER 19: WHO SINNED?

◆ ◆ ◆

And as Jesus passed by, he saw a man which was blind from his birth. And his disciples asked him, saying, Master who did sin, this man, or his parents, that he was born blind? Jesus answered, neither hath this man sinned, nor his parents: But that the works of God should be made manifest in him.

JOHN 9:1-3

Typically, when a believer or even a worshipper sees a person in a very challenging position, be it blindness, handicapped, or in poverty, they immediately jump to the conclusion that the person sinned and is not in a proper relationship with God, or when a prayer is not answered that God is having intractable difficulties forgiving them of a certain sin. I say this with great humility and respect that only a biblically ignorant person could embrace such a doctrine insofar as the thinking is foreign to scripture, in particular, Hebrews 8:12 which says, "for I will forgive their transgressions and their sins I will remember no more."

Since we know that God is not a petty God, His thinking is not like ours. We know His Son paid for our sins in full, so why are certain people in these conditions? The Master Teacher answered that perfectly when He said, "Neither this man nor his family sinned but that the works of God might be magnified through him." If you read the entire chapter of John 9, after much reviling and harassment by the religious folk (people who thought they knew God) Jesus encountered the blind man and asked him, "Do thou believe that I am the son of God?" The man answered, "Who is He Lord that I might believe on Him?" Jesus said, "Thou hast both seen Him and it is He who talketh with thee." The man replied, "Lord I believe," and he began to worship Him.

Recently while facilitating a homeless men's meeting, one of the facilitators states to the audience that instruction from God will make you wise and wealthy. I respectfully made a commentary humbly behind the speaker that the wisdom was guaranteed but not the wealth. My reason for the correction was because in the ministry, we try to teach the sincere milk of the word. After all, it is dangerous to tell a person to believe in what God did not promise. He promised that He would fulfill all the believers/worshipper's needs according to His riches in glory.

Another facilitator jumped up and shouted, "Well, how about the prodigal son?" I replied, "What made him prodigal?" The crowd answered, "He received his money too soon." The very next day I was accused secretly of teaching heresy and that is the reason why I'm not rich. During that time I was facing some financial challenges, nevertheless, God kept His promise proven to me by me being able to pay every bill and live in comfortable surroundings, but I was cursed in his eyes because I didn't have a Bentley or BMW like I did when I lived in Satan's kingdom and therefore the word of God was against me. What wasn't observed is, God was using that light affliction to get this book out to the public. So, when the religious thought that I had sinned and was cursed by God, God was using that opportunity to get His glory.

If this blind beggar was not in his condition, he more than likely would never have known God as the religious doubters. A person can't just come to God and worship; God makes worshippers before they come. When God is worshipped, He is worshipped through experience.

Many times, you will hear worshippers say things like, "I give you glory." If I get really deep, they will say, "I give you Gloooooory!" What's telling is, most are clueless of what God's glory is or how God gets glory through believers.

The Bible says in John 6:44, "Nobody can come to Christ unless the Father draws them." How does God draw a believer? The answer: through tribulation. Tribulation builds character, character is confirmed by experience, experience builds faith, and the result of faith always gives God glory. When a crack addict becomes a therapist, when a prostitute becomes a virtuous woman, when a thief becomes a person of integrity, when a cheating spouse becomes a faithful one, God gets His glory. But you have to go through it to get to it.

In conclusion, no one sinned, but it was a set up from the getup and the purpose was for God to get His glory. Glory is always followed by worship.

> When Jesus heard that He said, this sickness is not unto death, but for the glory of God, that the Son of God might be glorified thereby.
>
> JOHN 11:4

CHAPTER 20: SHOULD I
OR SHOULDN'T I?

◆ ◆ ◆

"Oh my God, I cry out in the daytime, but thou hearest not, and in the night season, I am not silent."

PSALMS 22:1

King David articulated a lament that most believers and worshippers go through during a point in their new life with God. David said that he cries in the daytime and God doesn't hear, and at night he does the same thing.

When I began to write this chapter the Holy Spirit of God named this chapter, "Should I or Shouldn't I?" "Should I or Shouldn't I?" is a spiritual part in a believer/worshipper's life that is tested randomly concerning worship. Enumerated below are three main reasons why believers/worshippers may not want to go to worship:

1) Do not want to sit under the word because it is convicting. Example: You just got out of bed with him/her and today's message is about fornication.

2) The preacher is boring or clueless. Example: You are going through a faith trial with your household being out of order and the preacher is preaching about whether a woman should wear pants or braid her hair.

3) You are in a season you don't even know that you're in. The enemy told you that God does not hear your prayers and you fell for it. Then the free will question pops up,

"Should I or Shouldn't I?"

I've found in my observation that in the kingdom of God, believers/worshippers are not honest about their emotions and feelings with God or about God. I recently had the experience of fellowshipping with a young lady named Lisa Cofield. Lisa is a beautiful African American woman with impressive academic credentials. By the nature of God, Lisa is a God chaser. She is not religious, but boy does she have a relationship with God. Many times, when Lisa is challenged, she consults me for spiritual advice. During the consultation, Lisa will say things like, "Listen, I have beef with God, I am not feeling this, I don't like that, and God and I are going to talk." Wow! At first, a person would say, "She's cocky, she's arrogant, she needs to humble herself." My spirit said she is full of faith. She is calling God on His word because she has demonstrated that she believes His word and I can say with all truth, after every rant that she has with God, it always ends in worship. "God is so good; God is so faithful. I just love me some Him."

When a person is in a "Should I or shouldn't I?" position, the enemy is having a full-blown conversation with the saint. What is telling is, the saint, who is a worshipper/believer, is considering what the enemy said.

When a person worships God, it should never be done by duty; rather, it should be done by devotion. When God receives worship, He doesn't force worship on you. He draws you to worship. When a person is drawn to worship, he or she is never drawn by the in-crowd (fraternity), his or her car, or by his or her feet, they are drawn in by their hearts.

Friday night, Saturday night, or whatever the night is before you worship, begin by asking yourself the question, "Should I or shouldn't I?" Understand and know that you are in a bad spiritual state. If you have a good Bible-believing preacher and he speaks as the Spirit gives him utterance but you question worship, you are in a serious spiritual state. Does that make you a bad person or a sinner? The answer is no because you have free will. The true problem is you have believed the enemy's report.

When you begin looking at God and take the focus off the issue or condition, your desire to worship comes back. When God introduced Himself to Moses, He told Moses that His name was the Great I Am, which translates to the God of the past, present, and future. This means that things you have discounted God for are still on the table. God says in Jeremiah 1:12, "I watch over my word to perform it." So, while you are being duped by the enemy, God is watching His word to bring your prayer to fruition.

Whenever you are sitting in worship service and that voice starts to talk to you and say, "I wonder who's preaching today. I don't feel like God today; it's cold, it's too hot, should I or shouldn't I, God hasn't moved, I cry day and night and nothing happens, it's a waste of time," just remember that it's the enemy that is continually trying to discourage you not to go to the house of worship, and the reason he is so adamant about discouraging you is that he knows your blessing is in the house.

Not forsaking the assembling of ourselves together, as the manner of some is; but exhorting one another: And so much the more, as ye see the day approaching.

HEBREWS 10:25

CHAPTER 21: YOU THOUGHT
THAT I WAS STUPID
(TWISTED WORSHIP)

◆ ◆ ◆

"But seek ye the kingdom of God and His righteousness and every-thing will be added."

MATTHEW 6:33

In the kingdom of God, the enemy has God's people blinded, distracted, frustrated, and confused, and the biggest tool he uses for the masses is money. When the believer begins to seek God, he seeks God's hand as opposed to God's face. Exactly what does that phrase, "seeking God's hand and not His face" mean? It means this: that when a believer begins to seek God, Christ gives clear instruction to seek the kingdom first. What are the things of the kingdom? 1 Timothy 6:6-11 gives us a glimpse of the things of the kingdom: "But godliness with contentment is great gain. For we brought nothing into this world, and it is certain we can carry nothing out. And having food and raiment let us be therewith content. But they that will be rich fall into temptation and a snare, and into many foolish and hurtful lusts, which drown men in destruction and perdition. For the love of money is the root of all evil: While some converted after, they have erred from the faith and pierced themselves through with many sorrows. But thou, O man of God, flee these things and follow after righteousness, godliness, faith, love, patience, meekness." Then it warns us to flee chasing after money because those who desire to be rich fall into temptation–a trap many foolish and hurtful lust after–and it drowns men in perdition.

You might ask, Where are you going with this and what does

it have to do with God's worship? My answer is everything! You can't serve God and money, as it says in Matthew 6:24: "No man can serve two masters: For either he will hate the one, and love the other; or else he will hold to the one, and despise the other. Ye cannot serve God and mammon." The enemy knows this to be true as well. And since you can't do both, you fail to worship Him in the manner that He ordained worship and that is in spirit and truth.

When the enemy has you with one foot in the kingdom and one in the world, you become a bipolar believer or a spiritual derelict. You become so deluded you begin to think that God thinks like you and you cannot even discern the voice of God. In that crazed state, you cannot get a financial breakthrough or any kind of leap forward because you never acknowledge God in worship for the prior acts that He has done. In worship lies the breakthrough.

Recently I observed one of the biggest lies that believers tell God. I ask you to give me a spiritual high five if you've heard it before. That lie is: "God, I want to be rich so that I can be a blessing to the kingdom." God's response" "Ok, how have you blessed the kingdom with what you have now?" If you can't answer that question, you have just lied to God. In truth, you want to be rich because you are tired of being poor. Poverty is loathing, shameful, and embarrassing.

While it appears that I am sitting on the judgment seat of Moses and condemning believers along with teaching a doctrine of poverty, I assure you that I am not. Rather, everything I just exposed I experienced in my walk with Christ, and it was one of the worst experiences of my lifetime. I had money but no peace. Not only did I lie to God, but I lied to myself and said that God said it. Just like He said in His word, it was a trap, a snare, and it pierced me through.

In the broken state that I am currently in, the enemy doesn't have the weaponry he had before. If my lights are off, you get worship. If my health fails, you get worship. If I am persecuted on my job, you get worship. If my finances are challenged, you get worship.

How can we be profitable to God and give Him glory being in the state of depression, stressed, and perplexed? This is not the life that God called believers into; rather, He called us into a life of perfect peace and complete joy. All of that is obtained in worship. You see, worship is not just for God, it's actually for you. Every time you enter His presence, something must change. The real question is, "Whose presence are you entering into?" God by His very nature cannot fail you and must bless you because if He doesn't, we have worshipped Him in vain.

Recently I was studying Israel and was reading Zechariah 2:8 which says, "He who touches you touch the apple of my eye." To short circuit the revelation God is saying, my Son has to come back to Israel to fulfill every promise that mankind's heart desires. If His feet don't land on the Mount of Olives, my word becomes void to humanity and my salvation plan is meaningless. If my salvific plan fails, life has no meaning.

I recently went on YouTube and the word of God is being fulfilled as I'm writing this book. I predict by the signs in scripture that Israel will be attacked between September 2019 and April 2022. The worshippers of God are not only sleeping but they are snoring. Preoccupation with the things that God didn't promise has believers choked out, and you cannot worship in a chokehold. Who has sat today and took an hour out of his or her day to pray for Israel; to minister to God concerning this horrific event that is going to take place very soon; to tell God that you stand with Him and you feel His pain?

We are so consumed that we never look at the end of Matthew 6:33 where it says, "and all these things shall be added." What are these things? These things are finances, assets, and status. Why would God withhold these things? Simple: God is not stupid. He understands man's spiritual condition and knows that man will attribute worship to an idol if man's spirit is not converted.

You reach a spiritual point in God that when you begin meditating and lusting after His Spirit the things that you stressed over and lusted after are presented to you in abundance, but you are so caught up in the spirit that you forget you even prayed for these things.

It is so crucial to be mindful of the things of God. Jesus referred to Peter as "Satan" when Peter cut the soldier's ear off. Jesus said, "Get thee behind Me Satan, because you are not mindful of the things of God."

The questions at bar are, what am I doing wrong and what are the things of God? Am I to be poor, visionless, sick, etc.? God forbid. To find out the things of God, you must first know the will of God. God said in 2nd Peter 3:8, "My will is that none perish but all come to repentance." When you read that verse and begin to apply it to your life, and then you are consumed by a relationship, a job, a business, a past offense, money, etc., you become virtually useless in the kingdom because your mind cannot be set on things above and below at the same time.

So, what is the conclusion of the matter? Simple: separate the things of God and the system of this world. Sanctify yourselves!

God has placed laws on this earth. Here are some examples:

Physical Law: If you eat a balanced diet and incorporate exercise you will live a long healthy life.

Moral Law: If you continually have unprotected sex with multiple partners, you will catch a disease.

Spiritual Law: Nobody comes to the Father except through the Son.

Financial Law: Work, pay your bills, dwell in a house consistent with your income, drive a car that is consistent to your income, be a good steward with that you have, make wise investments, work your investments with the spirit of excellence and your result, you will either be comfortable, rich, or financially free. No seed sowing, no Palma worms or cankerworms, no pressed down, shaken together and running over or the like, just natural application of the laws that God gave to the just and the unjust.

Mark Zuckerberg, Floyd Mayweather, Oprah Winfrey, Jay-Z, and Donald Trump are not Bible-thumping businesspeople, yet they possess great wealth. Why? Simple application. God rains on the sinner and the believer. It is a simple, practical application of the laws of finance.

When God begins to create a worshipper, the first thing God will give the worshipper is His peace. Why? God's peace is the beginning of worship. When God begins to pour His word in the worshipper's spirit to transform his/her mind, the worshipper begins to glorify God.

Recently I was preparing for work and as I was about to walk out the door, the morning news ran a story about a well-known televangelist investigated by the IRS for tax evasion. What was telling is that the preacher refused an interview and refused to be transparent with the IRS. Question: where is the holiness, righteousness, the peace? How can one worship while meditating on their shame being exposed? How can one worship with dirty hands? How can one worship God while trying to get out of a mess? The answer: you can't.

God said life in the Holy Spirit is righteousness, joy, and peace. This is illustrated in Romans 14:17: "For the kingdom of God is not meat and drink; but righteousness, and peace, and joy in the Holy Ghost." The enemy had twisted God's words and twisted the believer's minds until he gave us a spirit of stupor. In return when we approach God, we believe that He is like us, stupid.

As I began to close out this chapter, to give a more exhaustive revelation of stupor, I was led to a show on TBN where the preacher appeared to be a good man. However, he used the all-too-familiar trick on the saints that I coin as soothsaying. During his dissertation, he cleverly appealed to the heart issue of the believer and he began soothing them by flushing out the painful emotions of their issues. Once he began to get some amens and agreement, he did a very telling thing: he promised them that today was the last day they would deal with that issue if they sowed a seed. In their desperation, the saints began writing checks.

The Bible says in the book of Acts 16:16 that soothsaying can be profitable, and today it is more profitable than it was in the past. Wake up, believers and worshippers! God is not stupid or petty. Begin meditating on His wondrous acts in your life and begin worshipping Him. Shake off those false, dangerous doctrines and begin entertaining the secret place of the highest.

CHAPTER 22: FATHER, IN THE NAME OF FACEBOOK

◆ ◆ ◆

And lest thou lift up thine eyes unto heaven, and when thou seeth the sun, and the moon, and the stars, even all the host of heaven, shouldest be driven to worship them, and serve them which the LORD thy God hath divided unto all nations under the whole heaven.

DEUTERONOMY 4:19

When God gave Moses the law, He gave him very careful instructions: "to love the Lord thy God with all your heart, soul, and mind." In Deuteronomy 6:4-6 and Deuteronomy 4:19, He pointed out things that will cause you to draw to worship.

Recently on Facebook, I observed an evangelist that was going through some tribulation in her body. She began speaking to the Facebook audience as if she was speaking to God. She stated: "Facebook I'm sick; Facebook, I'm going to the doctors; Facebook, I just vomited; Facebook, I'm in the doctor's office; Facebook, the doctor will be calling me in a few minutes; Facebook, I took the test; Facebook, I have to wait two days for my results."Two days later she posted, "Thaaannnkkk you Facebook, I'm healed!" While this was an isolated incident, the behavior is going viral with believers, indicating God's worship is being replaced with social media. When you walk into most houses of worship, you will notice there are no longer Bibles. We are reading from cell phones, tablets, iPads, and the like. Scripture says in Hebrews 10:7, "Lo I have come in the volume of the book." I have personally observed pastors going on Facebook before they preach, and the congregation on the book during service.

Scripture warns us not to gaze at any images or constellations because it will cause us to worship that object. While I like social media and think that it has great assets, it can be dangerous for a worshipper.

When most believers begin to worship God, they call Him by different names that He manifested His glory through: Jehovah Rophe, Jehovah Shalom, Jehovah Nissi, etc., but one name you rarely hear is Jealous. Exodus 34:14 says, "For thou shall not worship no other god: For the LORD, whose name is Jealous, is a jealous God." Yes, God is a jealous God and He must be sanctified above anything on this earth. When you think of the term "jealous" you immediately think of something evil, but there are two kinds of jealousy. You have sinful jealousy, or desiring something someone else has with evil intent, and then you have righteous jealousy, which means God is eager to protect what belongs to Him alone. By nature, we are created to worship Him.

If you've ever flown over the Grand Canyon or Niagara Falls to view their opulence, you have visualized a small glimpse of God's majesty. When you look at the complexity of the human body, its architecture and the wiring of such, you observe the wonders of God's handiwork. Whenever you watch "National Geographic" and observe the many species of mammals, reptiles, amphibians, and fish, and think about how they reproduce, their defensive mechanisms for survival, their habitat, etc., one can only direct worship to the entity that caused these things to come into existence.

When a worshipper gets out of bed in the morning and the first thing they do is reach for their cell phone, they are attributing worship to an idol. When a worshipper spends the bulk of his or her day on social media, they are committing idol worship. When a worshipper is more intimate with anything on earth more than the God of Abraham, Isaac, or Jacob they have committed idol worship.

While I may come under strong criticism for my theology, I

can back it up scripturally. The Lord said in Matthew 6:9, "After this manner therefore pray ye: Our Father which art in heaven, hallowed be thy name..." What does it mean to hallow God's name? The perfect example is in 2nd Chronicles 20:6 which states: "And said, O Lord God of our fathers, art not thou God in heaven? And rulest not thou over all the kingdoms of the heathen? And in thine hand is there not power and might, so that none is able to withstand thee?" This prayer is markedly different from the evangelist's prayer.

God's name is set apart, meaning associated with nothing that came into creation. His attributes and geographical locations are set apart. Once He is hallowed, then worship begins. When worship begins, miracles are manifested, visions brought into fruition, and relationships restored.

> *Neither is there salvation in any other: For there is none other name under heaven given among men, whereby we must be saved.*
>
> ACTS 4:12

CHAPTER 23: QUIET!
"EMPIRE" IS ON

◆ ◆ ◆

I am the Lord; that is my name, and my glory will I not give to another, neither my praise to graven images.

ISAIAH 40:8

I recently observed people's responses to the television series "Empire." This is not a judgment because I do not have the authority to judge. It is purely a spiritual observation. I am an educator and noticed that the morning after my students watch "Empire," it takes them approximately 30 minutes to settle down and prepare for class. I am not angered or frustrated, but I am amazed to see their emotions so aroused. In the evening during my second job where I work as a behavioral health technician, I work on a women's unit that is customarily busier than I-95 in Philadelphia on the 4th of July. However, this particular night was the final episode of "Empire," and you could hear a pin drop on the unit. When I logged onto social media, I noticed that several church officials, bishops, pastors, deacons, and the like saying things like, "Don't call me between 8 pm and 9 pm, 'Empire' is on," "Getting ready for 'Empire,' text me later," "I'm glad this is the last episode of 'Empire,' now we can continue Bible study and worship service."

Let me first preface by saying that, as a minister and theologian, I believe in freedom in faith, and that life in the Holy Spirit is joy and peace. I would never attempt to dictate to a person where he or she should go, what they should eat, what they should watch on television, etc. That is called religious bondage. Nevertheless, I am gifted to be sensitive to the spirit of Almighty God.

Recently I counted how many times the word "glory" appears in the Bible, and it appears over 300 times. Because it appears so much, it demonstrates that God has great concern about His glory and that believers and worshippers should be sensitive concerning this attribute.

When getting worked up in praise and worship, we frequently say things to God like, "Lord I honor you; you are first in my life; I lay before you; I worship you." In reality, you intentionally come late to worship service, you sleep in church, or you text in church. In all actuality and truth, it's "Empire" or the other empire in your life that you honor (shutting down all communication 15 minutes before the show started). You gave glory (you discussed how wonderful the show was all week). You focused. You lauded before the show (because you never went to sleep and waited for a commercial before you relieved yourself in the bathroom). Does that make you a bad person? No, and God forbid. Jesus did not come to make bad people good; rather, He came to make dead people alive.

Why did I go through all of these convicting illustrations? Simple. When a believer, non-believer, or worshipper ascribes worship to anything apart from God, you're stealing what He said He wouldn't share, and that is His glory.

Whenever the glory of the Lord appeared in scripture, there was always a victory, blessing, healing, prospering, etc. Also whenever His glory appeared, there was an atmosphere for His glory to reside or hover over. How can a holy God come into an atmosphere where you constantly steal His glory? Your little empires in your life take priority over Him and He is honored, worshipped, focused on, or talked to second or third. Then you testify that God didn't answer your prayer. Question: How could He answer something He never heard?

Now we know that God heareth not sinners: But if any man be a worshipper of God, and doeth His will, him He heareth.

JOHN 9:31

Faith is not asking God for something, believing it will come to pass, and receiving it. Faith is also being sensitive to the Spirit of God and when you entreat Him regarding Him as Holy.

I am not on a campaign to slander the TV show "Empire"; I am, however, on a campaign to raise the sensitive consciousness of a holy God–the same God that sent stage IV cancer into remission. The same God that took you and your child off of drugs. The same God that took you out of the shelter and into your own house. The same God that, after the death of a loved one that you felt you couldn't make it without, healed your heart.

> *I am the Lord: That is my name: And my glory will I not give to an-other, neither my praise to graven images.*

> ISAIAH 42:8

CHAPTER 24: IF THESE KEEP QUIET

◆ ◆ ◆

The scene is the triumphal entry. Jesus is riding on a donkey into Jerusalem, among people spreading their cloaks on the ground in front of Him and shouting praises to God: "Blessed is the King who comes in the name of the Lord."

Some of the Pharisees (Jewish preachers) in the crowd said to Jesus, "Master, rebuke your disciples." Jesus replied, "I tell you if these will be quiet the rocks will immediately scream out." Most theologians read the passage and interpret the scripture figuratively as if to say the rocks crying out are the stones from the temple which would represent judgment for the Jews, but I roundly disagree because the operative word in that passage is "immediate." The Jews' judgment didn't come until decades later.

To add further credence to my theory, in the book of 1 Samuel 5:1-7 the Philistines took the Ark of God and set it in the House of Dagon. Right next to Dagon–a dumb idol with a face of a human–was a head like a fish that was worshipped by early Semitic people. The next day, Dagon was fallen upon on his face to the earth before the Ark of the Lord. They took Dagon and set him in his place again, however, the next day they found Dagon in the same fallen position.

What is the point the author is trying to make? The answer: everything, whether animate or inanimate that comes into existence, must worship God. That is why Jesus said, "If these be quiet the stones will cry out." That is how magnificent His glory is.

My next theory, and you may or may not agree with it, is there is a part of God's being that is predicated on worship. Whoa! Well author, how did you come to such a lofty, complicated theological conclusion? The answer is, through much prayer, meditation, and the study of the laws of cause and effect. Cause and effect says that nothing happens by blind chance or outside the universal laws. Every action has a reaction, or put another way, every cause has an effect and every effect becomes the cause of something else or greater.

So, when God made man in His likeness and image, it was a cause. What was the cause? The cause was to replicate Himself. Ok then, what is the effect? Worship. The only entity on this earth that can give God the worship that He thrives off of is something made in His image and likeness. A lion cannot worship God like a human because the lion is not wired like God; only a human is wired like God and can appeal to God's being. Moving forward, the necessity of worship sustains God's existence.

In Psalm 51:12 it says, "If I was hungry, I would not tell thee: For the world is mine and the fullness thereof." What is the Holy Spirit attempting to tell humans about God? The answer: God gets hungry. What does He get hungry for? The answer: Worship. Was God speaking paradoxically, parabolically, or anthropomorphically? No. He was speaking literally. Well, how can you say this with such certainty? Easy, connect the scripture. In Exodus 32 God killed 3000 Hebrews in one day. Why? Because they offered a calf for worship.

The word "kindled" appears in the scriptures at least 90 times, and 98% of the time it appears in the Old Testament. It is always used to describe God's anger, and it always resulted in death. Why was God's anger kindled? Because worship was ascribed to something other than God and His glory was given to another.

Moving further, there are two types of worship. There is what's called intrinsic worship where a human worships God naturally by nature. In short, I worship you because of who you are. Then there is salvific worship, when you worship God for what He did or how He met your need in the time of trouble. The difference between the two is that one is by duty and the other is by devotion.

When a man worships God by duty, he worships based on what

he is told to do because of common command. When a man worships God by devotion, he worships God based on love. Love has no commands or boundaries, so I may think about God in the morning, begin worshipping Him that afternoon, and then worship Him again in spirit for the next two months. Have you ever had a day where all you think about is God? You text, Skype, and post about God. Well, that is worshipping by devotion.

This type of worship moves the hand of God and activates His covenants. When His covenants are activated, there is always a prayer answered out of it.

So, don't keep quiet. A closed mouth won't get fed. Remember, if you keep quiet the rocks will cry out. Let's make some NOISE!

Make a joyful noise unto the LORD, all ye lands.

PSALMS 100:1

CHAPTER 25: THIS LIGHT
AFFLICTION

◆ ◆ ◆

W hen you begin to read the scriptures concerning the Jews, a biblically unlearned person would probably conclude that God was prejudiced concerning the rest of the non-Jewish population.

> "You are a holy people to God; and the Lord has chosen you to be a peculiar people unto Himself above all the nations on the entire earth."
>
> DEUTERONOMY 14:2

> "For the Lord has chosen Israel as a peculiar people for Himself."
>
> PSALM 135:4

When you read the history of the Jewish people, there is one common thread that they dealt with and that is affliction. Affliction: Something that causes great pain or suffering.

In November 1938, a 17-year-old named Herschel Grynszpan, a Jewish youth from Germany, was visiting his uncle in Paris. While there, he received a postcard informing him that his father, who had lived in Germany for 27 years, had been deported to Poland. Grynszpan in retaliation shot a German diplomat who was living in Paris. When the Nazi leaders heard the news of the shooting, they used it as a pretext to launch a violent attack against the Jewish community. On November 9, Nazi storm troopers attacked Jewish homes, businesses, and synagogues across Germany and Austria, murdering 100 Jews. They rounded up an additional 30,000 Jews and put them in concentration camps where two-thirds of them perished. That awful night was named "Kristallnacht" (the night of broken glass) after the Germans going through the neighborhoods smashing the windows of Jewish businesses.

This period was dubbed "the Holocaust," the mass extermination of six million Jews and five million others that were judged as inferior by the Germans. After the Holocaust, it was estimated that Hitler's Germany had executed 6000 Jews daily, including women, children, and infants. The lives of those who survived the concentration camps were changed forever, according to survivor Elie Wiesel. He has been quoted as saying: "Never shall I forget the small faces of the children whose bodies I saw transformed into smoke under a silent sky. Never shall I forget those flames that consumed my faith forever. Never shall I forget those moments that murdered my God and my soul and turned my dreams to ashes. NEVER!"

When you begin to read this chapter, it causes one to pause and start to ask God a set of serious questions. Are you God? Is faith a hoax? Is this a game? Why us? Why now? Do you hear our cry? Are you dead? How could you witness this and do nothing? Three phrases come to mind when pondering these questions: Intractable difficulty–hard to process through normal thinking. Insuperable difficulty–a situation that is impossible to figure out or understand. And the final one is mental gymnastics–difficult and complex logical thought. When these scenarios take place, you are at the height of spiritual warfare. Intractable difficulties, believing the word of God. Insuperable difficulties, attempting to see your way out of the situation. To round it out, you don't have the mental gymnastics to logically process this crisis, specifically because Almighty God's word is true and His promises must come to pass. But your situation in real-time is the very opposite of what God promised.

While that was the Jews' condition, Elie Wiesel had intractable, insuperable difficulties believing that God's word would continue to stand through the Holocaust. Wiesel won the 1986 Nobel Peace Prize and the Congressional Gold Medal. He never dreamed that he would author 57 books and impact the world through his sufferings during the Holocaust.

I also know that, while in death camps, Elie Wiesel and others in the Jewish nation didn't have the mental gymnastics to believe that right after the Holocaust, they would come out repossessing their land from which they had been displaced for over 1900 years. While in the death camps, their minds could not fathom the amount of worldwide success they would achieve owning–CNN, MSNBC, Fox News, New York Times, Washington Post, Dunkin Donuts, Baskin Robbins, Fannie Mae, Estée Lauder, Facebook, Google, Häagen-Dazs, Hasbro, H&R Block, Lane Bryant, Goldman Sachs, Snapple, Starbucks, Toys "R" Us, Warner Brothers, DreamWorks, Slim Fast, Calvin Klein, Dell, Apple, and a pantheon of other major successful business too numerous to name. I would have to author another book just to name them all. What is the point I'm attempting to make, what is God saying in His infallible word? This light affliction cannot be compared to the glory that will be revealed. He is saying to the believer, this suffering that you are presently enduring is absolutely nothing compared to the plan that I have in the end.

Recently while perusing social media, I came across a post from another pastor who is a friend of mine. He had posted a picture of the "middle passage." The middle passage is a time in history where African slaves were taken from Africa and loaded onto ships. The slaves were shackled together side by side in deplorable living conditions that were deemed one of the most despicable tragedies in human history. Slaves were shackled together for months at a time where they endured urinating, defecating, and regurgitating on one another. When they became ill, their European tormentors threw them overboard to be eaten by sharks. When they arrived at their destinations they were packaged for sale like cattle and forced into free labor. When I responded to his post, I captioned it, "this light affliction." My friend, this holy ghost-filled pastor replied sensibly, "I don't call this a light affliction and neither does God."

The error that the pastor made is in Isaiah 55:8-9 which says: "For my thoughts are not your thoughts, neither are your ways my ways, saith the LORD. For as the heavens are higher than the earth, so are my ways higher than your ways, and my thoughts than your thoughts." What God is attempting to communicate to this pastor; to Kobe Bryant's family; to the saints that were bombed in the AME church in South Carolina; to the millions of people whose lives were lost from the Black Plague; to the victims of 9/11; the victims of COVID-19 and any other mass/individual suffering is, what you view as a tragedy or the worst thing that could happen in a person's life, God views as almost nothing. It's like a tuberculosis shot, and the nurse tells you you're going to feel a little stick. The reason God says "this light affliction" is that He sees your end. You are in the moment; He is in the future. This is why the scripture says in Matthew Chapter 5, "Blessed are those who cry now because they will laugh." Only a holy God has a divine plan to switch insatiable pain into eternal joy. The only way to do that is to give me something better that will not only heal the pain but cause me not to remember it again. The joy is so unspeakable.

> And God shall wipe away all tears from their eyes; and there shall
> be no more death, neither sorrow, nor crying, neither shall there be
> any more pain: For the former things are passed away.
>
> REVELATION 21:4

Example: Recently one of the greatest U.S. sports personalities, Kobe Bryant, and his daughter, Gianna, were tragically killed after leaving a worship service. When the news hit, the nation was stunned. Perplexity and grief were on the faces of many of his admirers. Most people began to question God. They began to query themselves thinking what his wife and children must be going through. In Revelation 7:9, the Bible gives us a clue of what we will look like when we return. The verse says: "After this

I beheld, and lo, a great multitude, which no man could number, of all nations, and kindreds, and people, and tongues, stood before the throne, and before the Lamb, clothed with white robes, and palms in their hands." God is saying, the loved ones you've lost, whether European, Asian, African, Indian, Spanish, Russian, American, or whatever nationality, will come back to this earth physically speaking the same language and having an identifiable body. Wow!

Fast forward to the Kobe situation. If Vanessa Bryant and family saw that Kobe and Gianna would physically never experience pain or death again, what was suffered on this earth will be completely irrelevant when their glory (physical presence) is revealed. To physically embrace the same Kobe and Gianna, hug, kiss, sup with them, and talk to them would erase the very memory of the tragedy of what happened. What an amazing God.

> *For I reckon that the sufferings of this present time are not worthy to be compared with the glory which shall be revealed in us.*

> ROMANS 8:18

CHAPTER 26: BY HIS STRIPES

◆ ◆ ◆

There is this odd theory in the kingdom of God that Christians don't get sick, and that theory couldn't be further from the truth. Hezekiah was sick, Elisha died of sickness, Paul was sick, Timothy was sick, and Jesus died from the fatal torment, which was a sickness.

The proper way to read Isaiah 53:4-5 is spiritual healing, not physical healing. While God is a healer, and I know personally because I have been healed of cancer and congestive heart failure within the last year, healing is not a guarantee but a provision according to God's will.

Some time ago in 2004, I was involved in a prison ministry in New York. One of the pastors asked for us to pray for his mother, who was 85 years old and in the final stages of cancer. The entire church went on a fast. For three days and three nights, we had no food or liquids, simply hardcore fasting and prayer with Isaiah 53:4-5 as our banner. The following week, the pastor missed service for some unbeknownst reason. The next week, he came into the church and preached a dynamic message. After the message, as he was shaking hands before walking out of the church, one of the ministers said, "By the way, how is Mom?" With a dejected look he responded, "She died last week." He scurried to the exit and as I looked back, I observed the faces of 50 men that were silently thinking to themselves, "God, you failed." Nevertheless, worship continued, and the eerie look of a deer caught in the headlights was present on all of the brothers' faces. Their faith was under pure fire. Approximately two weeks later, I found myself asking God some daunting questions. I even began to shake my finger at Him, and for approximately one year God was completely silent on the matter with not one iota of a revelation.

One day I was watching a documentary on the deleterious effects of cancer. As I began watching the show, it talked about the excruciating pain in your lymph nodes when they become inflamed. I remember the pastor telling us that his mother had swollen lymph nodes throughout her body, and how each one was likened to a toothache. That is when God began to reveal that all of our fasting and praying was not in vain. He spoke these words, and I will never forget it: "Lamont, I received your fast and prayer, and I was elated with the communion." He continued, "You have read that I am sovereign, but you have not believed that I am sovereign, or you would not have prayed amiss." He said, "As a sovereign God I have all power and I can do whatever want. Your church was praying and believing in ME for physical healing on the left side; she was praying to walk into eternity on the right side to escape all the pain and suffering. I was in the middle weighing out the petition according to My word. After weighing it out, I affirmed her prayer; she has no more pain and she is awaiting you in eternity. After all, what quality of life could she live if I would have physically healed her?"

Since the fall of creation, we have been living in a world where death has a perfect statistic, and that is one per person. I don't quite know what happened to Bishop Jakes' mother, only God knows. What I do know is that God received the glory. That incident should have driven Bishop Jakes to clean out of the ministry, but instead, he rose to higher levels. Faith is not asking God for something and receiving it; rather, faith is believing God for something, not receiving it, and continuing to believe until you receive it.

Finally, I should note that the healing in Isaiah 53:4-5 is communicating a spiritual healing of your sin that will result in a physical body that is the same race, same language–one that can hug, kiss, have intimacy, doesn't aging, have pain, or suffer. One that will ultimately never experience death again.

Where would we be without A CHRIST?

Heal me, O LORD, and I shall be healed; save me, and I shall be saved: for thou art my praise.

JEREMIAH 17:14

CHAPTER 27: WOW, HE DOESN'T LIKE ME EITHER

◆ ◆ ◆

Wherefore God also gave them up to uncleanness through the lusts of their own hearts, to dishonor their own bodies between themselves: Who changed the truth of God into a lie, and worshipped and served the creature more than the Creator, who is blessed forever Amen. For this cause God gave them up unto vile affections: for even their women did change the natural use into that which is against nature: And likewise, also the men, leaving the natural use of the woman, burned into their lust one toward another, men with men working that which is unseemly, and receiving in themselves that recompense of their error which was meet.

ROMANS 1:24-27

When people begin to read the Bible concerning homosexuality, it is a mistake of epic proportions to believe that God thinks of homosexuals as humans do. I have a family member that was notorious for substantiating his dislike for homosexuals by justifying it in 1st Corinthians 6:9: "No fornicator, nor adulterer, or homosexual will enter the kingdom of Heaven."

One day while he was reciting it, I asked him to read verse 10 which says, "nor thieves, nor drunkards." He asked me why I asked him to read that particular verse and I replied, "When you read that verse you see yourself in there. Didn't God deliver you from drugs and alcohol?" Immediately a light went off as if he were thinking, "Wow, we were in the same condemnation." As we began to move forward in our ministry, I observed that his wife's attitude towards homosexuals had changed as well.

Firstly, God never condemns homosexuals in a personal, mean-spirited manner, rather, He carefully defines the borders of human sexuality so our joy can be full. It does not take a dual masters degree in physiology to logically conclude that the human body is not designed for homosexual relationships. For example, my oldest sister, Barbara McLaurin, worked in the nursing field for almost 20 years. While driving her home from work one day, she described an encounter that she had with an HIV patient. When she began to speak of the graphic details of the patient's open wounds and how upon redressing them the bandages stuck to the wounds, causing the patient additional pain in an already catastrophic condition. As I drove, it was revealed to me when God said He hates homosexuality, it means things such as the consequences that hinder your joy and endanger your health that God hates.

Most preachers preach against homosexuality in a condescending manner, in a way that God does not. In the book of 1st Corinthians 6:9-10, the Spirit of God gave an illustration of who is not fit for heaven: fornicators, extortioners, liars, adulterers, and idolaters. A biblically unlearned person would say, "Wow God, well who can be saved?" When you look at the suffix "er" you think of a boxer and what he does. He practices boxing. What a lawyer does, he practices law. What a golfer does, he practices golf. So, it is not the repentant sinner that misses heaven. God's mercy on sinners is a mystery. First and foremost, Jesus never came to take away SIN. The scripture says He came to take away sin, but what it means is He came to take away the "sin disposition."

In other words, when you sin, the Holy Spirit bears witness that you are a child of God because it convicts you, or rather it gives you a conscience and a feeling of remorse or depression that you did wrong. In the manner that you respond to the sin (cry, meditate, go into a depression, and ultimately confess), God hears and forgives immediately. On the other hand, there is a person that sins against God, is fully aware of their sins, practices the sins without caution, and cause others to do likewise. This is called blaspheming the Holy Spirit. God gives you light, and if you respond to that light, He gives you more light. If you do not respond to the light and continue in darkness, you are "not choosing God," however, you just chose your eternity.

My studies about homosexuality, along with a book titled, The Truth About Human Sexuality: When Biology Meets Theology by Dr. Marilyn Miles, helped me greatly. It's taught me that there are two types of homosexuality. One is the predisposition to homosexuality from birth, and the second referred to as Romans 1:24 homosexuality. This verse reads as such: "Wherefore God also gave them up to uncleanness through the lusts of their hearts, to dishonor their bodies between themselves." This is the homosexual who was born heterosexual with affection and desire for the opposite sex most of their lives and for some unforeseen reason, decides to have intimacy with the same-sexed person with an excuse to suit their conscience. For example, if it is a woman she may say, "I decided to become a lesbian because men are no good," and man would say, "I am tired of women."

In Genesis 19:1-7 there is a story about the male angels that came to Sodom. The scripture said when the men of Sodom found out that they were at Lot's house, they began to pound on the door asking for sex from the male angels. Lot's response was, "I pray you brethren, do not so wickedly." Lot then offered the men his virgin daughters and the men refused.

Most people think wicked and evil are the same, but they are not. Evil is anything that God wouldn't do, and wicked is when a human commits an act that he or she knows is evil, understands the implications of such, and being fully aware that God hates it when they do it, they celebrate the action publicly. When that action is done, they are telling God that they reject salvation.

Some may ask, how you can prove that some people are born gay? The first thing I would suggest is to do your scientific research. There is a voluminous amount of empirical evidence to back up my claims.

Approximately 14 years ago I was talking with a good friend of mine who had a child out of wedlock. He would send me pictures of the child as early as 18 months and I could see the predisposition of female characteristics in this male child. When talking to the child's father a few years later, he said he had taken his son clothes shopping and he asked him for a pink dress. This is not learned behavior at the age of four, but rather a predisposition. The question would be, what is God's position on the predisposed homosexual? The answer is, we live in an imperfect world that fell the moment Adam sinned. Before Adam's sin, we lived in a world that did not have earthquakes, sickness, deformities, or sexual immorality. When a predisposed homosexual is born with unbalanced hormones, this is what usually happens. The question then becomes, can predisposed homosexuals act out on their inclination knowing that they were born this way? The answer is a resounding NO!

When a person is born with no arms, he/she by nature learns to use their feet in place of their hands to write, eat, play instruments, and the like. They do not resolve that because they are born that way that they are going to live out their lives with limitations because of their deformity. This is the same with homosexuals.

Approximately nine years ago I was working at a children's shelter in the Germantown section of Philadelphia and I encountered two residents, a young man and a young lady. The young man was perfectly effeminate, and the young lady was perfectly masculine. One day they both signed out to attend a neighborhood church service that most of the residents attended. When they returned, I asked them what each of them had learned in church and they said they were taught that through God's power, you do not have to be gay. I nodded my head as if to say, "good teaching" when in fact I did not believe it myself. As the weeks passed, I noticed a change in both residents. The young man would go out of his way to give me a firm handshake and spoke in deep voice modulation. At the same time, the young lady had abandoned her usual attire of basketball shorts for a more effeminate look. One day both were out on passes, and upon their return, as they walked towards the building's entrance, they were holding hands. The young lady's hair was curled, she had on lip-stick, she was wearing a skirt, etc., and the young man looked transformed as well. Because of boundaries, I kept the matter at heart. But what it led me to believe is, "With God, ANYTHING is possible!"

In conclusion, God does not condemn homosexuals or any other person for that matter. It is the actions of people that He condemns. When God says that He hates homosexuality, He is only carefully defining the borders of your sexuality so your joy can be fulfilled. God would NEVER send a person born in a struggle to an eternal struggle. It is just not His nature to do so.

> There is therefore, now no condemnation in Christ Jesus for those who walk not after the flesh but after the Spirit.
>
> ROMANS 8:1

CHAPTER 28: YOUR HANDS CANNOT HIT WHAT YOUR EYES CANNOT SEE: COVID-19

◆ ◆ ◆

Years ago, Boxing Hall of Fame great Muhammad Ali had a song with the lyrics, "I float like a butterfly, sting like a bee, your hands can't hit what your eyes can't see." Recently President Trump was describing COVID-19 as the invisible enemy, and it is.

Approximately 2000 years ago, the disciples came to Jesus on the Mount of Olives and asked a very telling question: "Jesus, tell us about the end of the world and your coming." Jesus began to prophesy and predict the future. In Matthew 7:24, Jesus predicted that there would be famines and plagues in various places. He then said in verse 8, "all these things are the beginning of sorrows."

Concerning COVID-19, there are a pantheon of theories alluding to it coming from bats in a laboratory in Wuhan China, to a laboratory in North Carolina, that it is a thrombosis (blood clots), God's wrath on humanity, and a whole host of other theories. If one is committed to truth, one would have to agree that this virus is a mystery with incomprehensible elements to it. Flat out, this means that mankind is perplexed and clueless on how to fix this pressing issue.

Recently I was watching CNN and a nurse was being interviewed about her experience with COVID patients. She was trembling and crying as she stated, "I had three patients, all of their vitals were stable. I stepped away for ten minutes and when I returned, all three of them were dead." As I observed the journalist Don Lemon, who is consistently stoic during his broadcast, he appeared to be having an out-of-body experience, pondering what the nurse had just shared with him.

A recent post on Facebook read, "If God was in control of everything, why wouldn't He just put an end to the Coronavirus?" Firstly, just because God knows a thing and has the power to stop a thing (which is called God's providence), this does not or should not define God to be responsible for COVID-19, or not ending it in a time frame that is reasonable to the human mind, and should not have one surmise that God is evil or vindictive. Rather, if one is wise and committed to the truth, if to date there have only been one million casualties worldwide and the total population is 7.8 billion, then when you do the math (.01% death rate), instead of charging God we actually should be thanking Him that the percentage is so low.

There is a question that humans always ask God without giving the question careful consideration and that is, "Why is there so much evil in the world?" The problem with the question is that it's posed incorrectly. The correct question should be, "Why is there so much goodness on the Earth?" Out of a population of nearly eight billion people, only a tiny fraction are murderers, drug dealers, pedophiles, rapists, arsonists, and the like. If God took His SPIRIT off the Earth, that number would be 100% across the board.

A verse in the book of Matthew 24:8 says, "these are the beginning of sorrows." While one would look at the George Floyd murder and suggest rioting around the world right after COVID was the beginning of sorrows, unfortunately, it is going to get much, more chaotic than that.

The presidency of Donald J. Trump, the outbreak of COVID-19, and the murder of Floyd, while tragic, are smokescreens or diversions so you will not see that which is coming. When you read further into the chapter, the Bible mentions or describes a person that He coins as" the abomination of desolation." Some of the scriptures refer to it as the antichrist, man of sin, or son of perdition. When the stage is perfectly set, this person will be revealed. According to the scriptures, the characteristics of this person will be a man very eloquent, easy on the eyes, very charismatic, and the total opposite of President Donald Trump. You may have some people rejoicing saying, "Hallelujah, Allahu Akbar, about time, thank you Lord," but when that person is revealed, it will make President Trump look like Martin Luther King, Jr.

In other words, this person may very well be looming on the horizon this very day and time. When he appears, he is going to be very, very appealing. The Bible says he will deceive the very elect, but once he is revealed, he is going to cause the greatest tribulation that mankind ever witnessed. I honestly believe that happenings like the Coronavirus and George Floyd's murder are going to usher this world into that false peace and after His time is up, God Himself is going to usher us into a perfect peace. One might ask, "How can you predict this based on the two isolated incidents?" The answer is this: while they were two isolated incidents, both spread around the world, especially the murder of George Floyd, who was a regular African American citizen who suffered a tragic ending by a white police officer, but for some unforeseen reason, he was given a Martin Luther King, Jr. type of tribute internationally which causes one to PAUSE. When we begin to see incidents that should give national unrest and it turns to international unrest, know for sure that the prediction of the antichrist prophesied in the books of Daniel and Revelation will come to pass.

In conclusion, a holy, righteous, and sovereign God is not just sitting around watching Corona and deciding to do nothing about it; rather, this holy, righteous, sovereign entity is in the process of turning this diabolical pandemic around for the good. The only positive out of Corona is that it is a virus with such perplexity that it causes humans to pause. During this "pause" men are facing trepidation (uncertainty), fear, apprehension, and anxiety. During that time, it is a recipe for SALVATION.

Salvation is life on planet Earth in which you have a physically recognizable body where you are the same race, speak the same language, never to deal with racism, cancer, lupus, diabetes, COVID, crack cocaine, heroin, Percocets, incarceration, funerals, graveyards, and finally, death.

So, in the grand scheme of things, COVID is traumatizing, painful, agonizing, depressing, and the like but unlike eternity, it has an end. At its epicenter, it is all a part of the grand scheme of God's magnificent plan that He has for eternity, although He had absolutely nothing to do with the inception of COVID. He will have everything to do with turning all of COVID's agony, trauma, and death into joy forevermore.

> And God shall wipe away all tears from their eyes; and there shall be no more death, neither sorrow, nor crying, neither shall there be any more pain: for the former things are passed away.
>
> REVELATION 21:4

CHAPTER 29: IF THERE IS
NO RESURRECTION....

◆ ◆ ◆

While I was teaching a class one day, a senior student asked a brilliant question: "Brother Lamont, what is the difference between resurrection and reincarnation?" Before I could answer, a sixth grader blurted out, "Reincarnation is a Hindu fantasy like Santa Claus and the tooth fairy. The resurrection is a historical fact." The entire class paused and simultaneously gave the sixth-grader a round of applause.

When I began to reflect on the young lady's answer, it made me think about this question that is posed to every human on the face of the earth at one time or another. The question is, "If there is no resurrection from the dead, does life make sense?" Some of the most brilliant people on the planet are atheists. Most atheists ask brilliant questions such as:

1) If God exists, why is there suffering?
2) If God saw slavery and did nothing about it, does not that make Him complicit?
3) Why would a just, holy, and righteous God see a disease that is going to kill 60% of a European continent and simply do nothing about it? (the Black Plague)?
4) Why would an all-knowing God see a pedophile, serial killer, or a rapist in the future and allow them to come into existence and harm innocent people?

Most people think atheists are obnoxious, haughty people, and some are. I think they ask some highly intelligent, common-sense questions that people of faith are scared to ask or confront God with. At the epicenter of most atheist, agnostic, Muslim, Jews, Jehovah's Witness, Hindu, Sikhist, Jainism, Zoroastrians, Shintoism, Taoist, Confucians, Mormon, or Catholic questions is the quest to make sense of life. In every religion on earth this question is addressed, and humans fail at attempts to answer.

One of the fastest-growing religions on earth is Islam. Recently a young lady that I was mentoring died from a drug overdose. She had been tormented for almost 15 years with this disease. I often saw her homeless, hungry, displaced, high, and downtrodden. When she died, she left five young children who are now orphans. I spoke to a friend of mine who is a devout Muslim, and as he began to pray it went like this: "May Allah make her grave spacious, fill it with light and forgive her for all of her sins and grant her Jannah (Paradise)." Let's attempt to humbly and respectfully make sense out of that prayer:

1) Why would God make your grave spacious?
2) How would God making her grave spacious give peace to her soul with all the hell she went through on earth?
3) If God makes the grave spacious, then the only hope is more dead bodies in it.
4) Forgiveness of sin requires a sin-bearer. Sin cannot be prayed for, it must be atoned.
5) May God grant her paradise. Paradise in Islam, according to Sura 55 Verse 65-75, is for men having intimacy with Houris or virgins, and the virgins are fair, or of light complexion or Caucasian. This person was of African descent so that disqualified her from PARADISE.

This is not a knock against Islam or any other religion. What I am attempting to illustrate is that empty sayings such as "Rest in peace," "May Allah make your grave spacious," "Mommy is with the angels," "Daddy is in heaven," "My baby sister is in a better place," unfortunately none of these clichés make soul-satisfying sense.

Death is a mystery with incomprehensible elements to it (not easy to understand). When the death of a human occurs, the tears shed are called a "soul cry." A soul cry is different from any other cry because you are shedding tears for the very existence of a person who doesn't exist anymore. That is when your soul begins to take up a travail. During that travail you don't know who to turn to, the pain won't subside, and you feel like you are dying inside. In the vicissitude of the heart lies hopelessness and perplexity. This is the point where you must encounter something outside of yourself.

A few years ago, one of the parents from my school lost her youngest child. One night her son came home, put something in the microwave, went upstairs, and fell asleep. While asleep he died. The next morning, they discovered that her son had left food in the microwave, and like a good African American mother she called to him, scolding him about leaving food in the microwave. When he did not answer she ascended the steps, walked into his room, and at that moment her life changed forever.

During the funeral, I began to spiritually study her travail (instrument of torture) and when she approached the casket, she let out a wail (high pitched inarticulate cry during grief) that no human agency could remedy to fix. What she wasn't aware of, even as I write this book, is that every Friday night around 3 am her son called me to have Bible study while I was at work. I can guarantee her that her son's soul was saved before he left this earth, guaranteeing him an eternal existence when he returns.

Approximately 2000 years ago, a dear friend of Jesus was dying. When Jesus was told about his death and was asked to hurry to save his life, Jesus made a two-day journey in the opposite direction. The purpose of a two-day journey in the opposite direction was to make certain that his friend Lazarus was not only dead but stinking. When a dead person stinks, it certifies and codifies that the person is dead. When Jesus finally arrived, He had a conversation with Lazarus' sister, Martha, and it went something like this: "Lord, if you had been here my brother would not have died." Jesus replied, "Your brother will rise again." Martha said, "I know in the last day, the resurrection." Jesus replied, "I am the resurrection and the life, He that believe on ME though he were dead, yet shall live. And whosoever liveth, and believeth in ME shall never die. Do you believe this, Martha?" If you observe the conversation between Martha and Jesus, He did not say He heard of the resurrection or that He believed in the resurrection; rather, He identified Himself as the resurrection. Then He proved it by raising Lazarus from the dead.

This is not a conscious attempt to evangelize, proselytize, convert, or get you to join a church; rather, it is an attempt to cause you to develop an eternal perspective on life and eternal existence. If we are committed to the truth (calling a red light red and a green light green), these colorful comforting sayings of "May the ancestors watch over them, may the universe give them direction, may Allah make your grave spacious, they are smiling down on us," does not address the fact that what you loved with all of your heart and soul ceased to exist. And the only thing that will satisfy or erase that feeling is if the non-existent began to exist again. Eternally! Period!

In the book of Revelations 13:8, it refers to Jesus as the lamb slain before the foundation or (beginning) of the earth. Why did God have to kill the Christ to restore man to God? Because although God knew that He made a perfect earth and a perfect man, He also knew that He gave man a free will. In man's freedom of will, He also knew that man was free to rebel against Him. In this rebellion, it would cause mankind to have a life span ending in death or non-existence. He also knew that the only way to reconcile, reset, fix, or redo this thing was to give eternal existence in another dimension on the same earth, and to give you back eternally every single physical thing that you ever treasured, loved, or adored. That could come only through one way, and that is Jesus the Christ.

The most ardent skeptic, Agnostic, Bible-bashing person in this world would have to agree that IF THERE WAS NO RESURRECTION FROM THE DEAD WOULD LIFE MAKE ANY LOGICAL SENSE?

If you take a study of every religion on the planet, each and every one has a common thread and that common thread is Jesus. If you take the resurrection out of Judeo-Christianity, the entire faith collapses. Therefore, while the theory is exclusive and not debatable the question at bar now is, is the resurrection a historical fact?

In our judicial system, two types of evidence will convict a defendant and they are factual and circumstantial evidence. When proving the resurrection, there are a core set of circumstances that logically conclude that 2000 years ago, a Jewish carpenter arose from the graveyard and continues to live this very day. Whenever a trial judge presides over a trial, he or she most often will instruct the jurors on how to come to a logical conclusion concerning circumstantial evidence. He will start by saying, "Ladies and gentlemen of the jury." Imagine it is the month of January around 6 pm and you are coming home from work. When you get home there is no snow on the ground and the skies are clear. You have dinner, shower, and go to bed. You sleep until 6 am the next morning, and when you get up and look out the window, there are seven inches of snow on the ground. While you didn't physically see it snow, by all logical deductions you came to the logical conclusion that it snowed overnight.

Now it takes more faith to believe that Jesus did rise from the dead than He did not. To believe that Jesus didn't rise from the dead, you would have to believe that a prophecy was written in Psalms 16:10, 1000 years before His appearance, then 1,000 years later what was predicted came to pass and you say it was a coincidence. You would have to believe that after sweating blood droplets, a condition called hemostasis (when you are so distressed that your blood capillaries burst causing blood to come out of your sweat glands adversely causing your skin to become very soft), so that when He was beaten with goat's bones (razor blades) His veins and blood vessels were sliced up causing severe bleeding.

After this, He was compelled to carry a 300-pound wooden cross approximately one mile. When He arrived at Golgotha, He was laid upon the cross and nails were put in His wrists and feet.

While He was suspended in air, He began to asphyxiate for six hours. During the last hour, a Roman guard took a spear and thrust the point into Jesus' fifth interspace of His ribs and immediately water and blood began to pour from the pericardial sac (the water encasing for the heart). This puncture was the size of a silver dollar in diameter.

They then took His body down and prepared it for burial-washing the body, stuffing it with spices, giving it an oil treatment, and then finally wrapping it. The body was then placed into a tomb on an incline with a 5000-pound stone with Caesar's seal placed in front of it. In those days, the penalty for compromising anything with Caesar's seal on it was crucifixion, upside down with your entrails coming out of your mouth. The entrails are then set on fire with the flames entering your body, causing instantaneous combustion. All these things happened to Jesus inside the tomb for three days with no medical attention. He then rose from the dead, rolled away that enormous tombstone, subdued trained armed guards, and strolled around Jerusalem with pierced hands and feet and a hole in His heart. His disciples ran out on Him pre-resurrection, but he seduced them into spreading the myth that He conquered death and lived out His pathetic life in obscurity.

I say this with great respect and humility, that if a person looks at the evidence for the post-resurrection and concludes that Jesus didn't rise from the dead, one would have to logically deduce that the person is disconnected from logic, reason, and reality.

To the parent who prayed for their child and lost them to a drug overdose; to the heroin addict that fought addiction for 50 years and died under a bridge; to the child that stood at the top of the steps and overheard the news that daddy is not coming home from the war; to the mom that lost an innocent toddler to a senseless drive-by shooting; to the parent that ran to the corner store and when they returned their house had burned to the ground with their children in it; to the person who was having casual sex and two months later the physician calls to announce they're HIV positive; to the mom and children whose husband/father that is a police officer, hugged him and said, "See you in the morning" only to wake up and find out on the news that daddy is never coming home again; to the person who was molested and must carry that pain every day because you fear the shame if it was ever exposed; to the thousands of cancer patients on Facebook ads, commercials, and Instagram ringing the bell and screaming, "I'm cancer-free" only to die three months later; to the 18-year-old whose mind told them to kill someone and now two years into their jail sentence, they realize that you will never take a bath, get married, have Thanksgiving dinner with the family, attend your parents funeral and you can't even remember why you pulled the trigger; to the dialysis patient whose blood must be transfused three times a week five times a day or they will die; to the lupus sufferer whose entire body is wracked with pain in their joints, organs, and epidermis; to all that I have mentioned and so many more, if God saw your pain, choices, and decisions and did not plan a RESET, REDO, RECOVERY or in a nutshell, a RESURRECTION, one would have to conclude that God is the most wicked, maniacal, demented, deranged, berserk, bloodthirsty, bipolar, schizophrenic entity known to mankind.

Because of the resurrection, one would have to conclude that He is all-wise, merciful, totally righteous, sovereign, holy, judicious, and the most extreme composition of love. To bring you out of nothing into something, give you freedom of will and opulent earth, made you master over it and gave you authority over it, we then turn around and begin living a total life of rebellion to a holy God and the grand expression of your love is to leave your cosmologically complex domain, come to this one for the express purpose for all that will believe in Him will exist again never to see non-existent.

Most religious people debate or argue about their religion or thinking about who God is, when what they are attempting to do is make pure logical sense out of life. The true conclusion that every sensible human being on the planet has to logically agree with, and in order for life to make sense, is that we have to exist again, never to be subject to death, disappointment, or anything that offends. So, the indisputable, immutable fact is, IF THERE IS NO RESURRECTION FROM THE DEAD, THEN LIFE DOES NOT MAKE ANY LOGICAL SENSE!

> *Then Jesus saith unto him, "I am the way, the truth, and the life: no man cometh unto the Father but by me.*

JOHN 14:6

CHAPTER 30: END GAME

◆ ◆ ◆

When I first began writing this manuscript, I told about ten people from diverse backgrounds and nationalities about the book. When they heard the title, the first thing they said was "Wow!" All paused and looked at me as if to say, "What is his end game?"

When I encountered God, I did not adopt a religious spirit or character; rather, I began to study the deep things of God like suffering, poverty, unrest, disease, death, and world religion.

My initial presence on social media is when I observed that a great many humans asked, pondered, or inquired the same questions that I pondered, but they came to a presumptive conclusion without a fair trial. The reason God was found guilty without a fair trial was because of the three dangerous words underscored below:

1) Perception: A way of understanding
2) Presupposition: When the person assumes on a thing based on limited information which shapes their world view on a thing or subject.
3) Presumption: An idea that is taken to be true, although it is not known for certain.

As a person of faith, I am an orthodox Judeo-Christian and as odd as my faith appears to be, so is my thinking. From a perception standpoint, most people think that when one comes to faith in Christ, life begins to instantaneously change for the better–houses, cars, health, long life, sound mind, and the like. That could not be further from the truth.

In Acts 9:16 when the Jewish terrorist apostle Paul had an encounter and met Christ, the first words or rather instructions out of Christ's mouth to His disciple Ananias was, "Arise and go to a street called Straight and meet with Saul of Tarsus and show him how many things he must suffer for my sake." In another verse, Jesus told His disciples, "Take up your cross and follow Me." The cross is symbolic of suffering unto death. So, when the average person looks at God from their perspective, they presumptively think of all things good, righteous, holy, and sovereign, never expecting an Apostle Paul experience, a Jesus experience, or an experience encountering a tragedy such as a motorcycle accident, diabetes, COVID, heart failure, lupus, a stray bullet killing an innocent person, or a child dying from cancer at St. Jude's Hospital for Children.

Approximately six years ago, my mentor, Elder Ernest Chandler, invited me to hear a man named Pastor Herman Washington speak. I accepted the invitation, and as I observed Herman Washington break down the book of Exodus, he uttered this statement that shook my foundation and birthed a book out of it, How Could I Worship You If I Can't Trust You. The speaker is a man filled with God's Spirit and has a zeal for God that is unmatched. At that time, he had traveled from New York to Philadelphia to give this word while mourning the death of his wife.

As I observed Reverend Washington, it appeared that in the vicissitude of his heart he had a bevy of serious questions for God that he kept at heart, out of respect for the relationship he had with God. While not certain of the questions Herman Washington had for God, I know on the way home that I examined God in the manner that a district attorney would examine a defendant in a Mafia case loaded with audio evidence. This man is Your servant, as Your servant he meditates on Your word day and night. He traveled from New York to Philadelphia to give a handful of poor people encouragement. When he returns to his neighborhood, he is a beacon of light for all who encounter him. So here is the question, Lord: his wife died, he prayed for her life, he believed You for her life, he is left with a son to raise alone and you had the power to bring another result. Why? Why? Why?

The answer is this: when God reveals Himself to mankind, He does it in part, not exhaustively. If God revealed Himself exhaustively then we would not have to live by faith because the hope that is seen is not hope. For if we see it, we no longer hope for it. To that end, some things are incomprehensible to the human mind because we cannot understand that, although we prayed healing for a loved one, God took them. You prayed for deliverance for a child who is in addiction, and they died from an overdose. You prayed for your marriage, but it ended in divorce. When scenarios like these occur and your prayer result is the direct opposite of your petition and God's word, then you must HOLD ON TO THE DEEP END OF GOD'S WORD–that is, to look at nature and say every day is day and every night is night. Every season is a season, every animal is unique in its habitat, the earth revolves around the sun 365 days a year and does not miss a beat, the Atlantic and Pacific oceans meet but do not merge.

When you begin to do your logical deduction, it all traces back to God. What that tells me about God is that He is consistent and faithful. Therefore, that must be a part of His character. Therefore, while I don't have the mental gymnastics to understand why the result of my prayer was the opposite of what my heart panted for, what I do know is that God is consistent, faithful, cannot lie, and as statistically accurate as His works are, so is the accuracy of His word.

I was recently watching a YouTube video of Reverend Herman Washington and he was preaching a message called "Reckoning the Faith." While I was watching the video, he said something very striking: "The Bible does not contain the word of God, the Bible IS the word of God." Herman has since remarried, his son is well, his ministry is prosperous, and while he may have preached about "reckoning the faith," he never lost it.

My ostensible purpose for writing this book was for the same questions that you ask of God in your own meditation, daydreaming, or the like, I have asked these very same questions. Two of the most devastating scriptures in the Bible are Proverbs

3:5-7 and Isaiah 55:8-9:

> *Trust in the Lord with all thine heart; and lean not unto thine own understanding. In all thy ways acknowledge Him and He will direct thy paths.*
>
> PROVERBS 3:5-6

> *For my thoughts are not your thoughts, neither are your ways my ways, saith the Lord. For as the heavens are higher than the earth, so are my ways higher than your ways, and my thoughts than your thoughts.*
>
> ISAIAH 55:8-9

Humans from all walks of life must begin to develop an eternal conscience when it pertains to the Creator of this universe. The reason the Creator says to lean not unto thine own understanding is because your understanding is limited. Therefore, you can only understand as far as the boundaries your limited mind will allow you to go. God is eternal and He is outside of creation, therefore, one must trust that if a Holy, righteous, sovereign, all-knowing God allowed a tragedy to be, just by the laws of cause and effect alone it must have a greater purpose.

When you go outside and you see the distance between heaven and earth, you might ask, what is the distance between heaven and earth? The answer is it is incalculable because heaven is beyond space and you attempt to measure God's thoughts against your thoughts, then you begin to develop what's called "an eternal mindset." Then the Creator can answer that daunting question, "how can I worship You if I can't trust You?" And God's response that He screams to humanity is:

"Trust ME when you cannot trace ME."

ABOUT THE AUTHOR

Lamont Mclaurin

Author Lamont McLaurin is a retired Greater Hope Christian Academy Theology Teacher from Philadelphia, PA. He devotes his time to mentoring chaplains at the University of Pennsylvania on Islamic Care. As a theologian, Lamont has authored several controversial books with hot button topics that provoke thought and often controversy.

McLaurin has studied alongside some of the greatest theological minds such as the late great Ravi Zacharias, Hank Hanegraaff, Lee Strobel, David Evans Jr., Jonathan Cahn, and the list goes on.

In this manuscript, McLaurin has accomplished what no theologian in history has done and that is to produce a book that humans of all races, creed, and culture can relate to. One that ceases and desist the debate about religion. A book that turns tragedy into hope and optimism. One that gives a clear logical meaning to life.

No matter where life finds you, you will never see your life, perspective of God, or "no God" the same after a thorough examination of this 21st Century Super Nova!

Made in the USA
Middletown, DE
25 June 2021